CHRISTIAN PRAYER THROUGH THE CENTURIES

Christian Prayer Through the Centuries

by

JOSEPH A. JUNGMANN

Translated by

John Coyne, S.J.

PAULIST PRESS
New York/Ramsey/Toronto

A Deus Books Edition of Paulist Press, originally published under the title *Christliches Beten*, copyright © 1969 by Verlag Ars Sacra Joseph Mueller, Munich, West Germany.

Library of Congress
Catalog Card Number: 78-61729

ISBN: 0-8091-2167-0

Published by Paulist Press
Editorial Office: 1865 Broadway, New York, N.Y. 10023
Business Office: 545 Island Road, Ramsey, N.J. 07446

Printed and bound in the
United States of America

Contents

Preface

Foremost among man's privileges is his ability to pray. He can enter into contact with his maker, can speak with him, give answer to him from whom he has received all that he has. The Church of God is the community of those whom he has called and who answer him in the language of prayer. This answer takes place chiefly at the church assembly where Christ himself is present in the midst of his members inviting them to share in his own sacrifice and prayer. Outside the assembly it occurs again and again when worshipers meet to pray together, or when a person retires to his/her room and prays to the Father in secret or raises his/her heart to God amidst life's struggles. Prayer accompanies the Church on her pilgrimage through this world and will not be silenced till the day of her final consummation. Being part and parcel of her wandering, prayer is also open to all the influences and vicissitudes which mark her path through this world. For that reason it is possible to write a history of prayer.

Such an undertaking constitutes a risk as in the last resort prayer remains a secret between humanity and its God. But if the venture meets with some measure of success, it will reveal to us a central factor in the Church's total history. There is, of course, a difference between the history of public prayer, the liturgy of the Church, and private, personal prayer. The former is a task to which, for some centuries past, capable writers have devoted their energies. Their task was made all the easier as they dealt with clearly defined forms, forms in which the law of reverence for tradition was specially operative. In the case of nonliturgical prayer, with which we are primarily concerned, the forms are much more varied and more difficult to assess, as the most authentic prayer takes place outside all forms, in the secret encounter between God and man/woman.

Hence it is invariably the externals of prayer alone that are accessible to us, the framework within which genuine prayer is carried on; or when that prayer finds its echo occasionally in other sources. In addition to such sources, which are numerous and reach back to fairly early times, we also have plenty of studies which throw light on individual facets in this long and chequered history of prayer. And though each source-text and each study taken by itself are welcome acquisitions, still it is only when they are arranged in a larger context that their full significance appears.

Such is the purpose we have in mind in the following inquiry, and yet there can be question here of a mere outline in which plenty of gaps and inaccuracies are bound to occur.

Questions To Be Asked

In tracing the course of Christian prayer through the centuries many questions have to be posed. First of all what was understood by prayer? Was it regarded as a steep ascent to God? As repose in God? As an anticipation of that possession of him to which we are all invited? Was it perhaps the fulfillment of an obligation to pray? Or did it serve as a surety of salvation? And if the latter, what role was assigned to the prayer of petition, and what to a confession of one's weaknesses and sinfulness?

As Christian prayer is based on revelation and is confined within the boundaries set by the Christian order of salvation, we may ask to what extent were such factors a reality in prayer at any given time? We shall come across periods when a rounded picture of the Christian world of faith was kept in view, other periods when only partial aspects of it were clearly prominent, when piety was nourished on meager rivulets of Christian thought and which nevertheless produced abundant fruits of sanctity.

On that question hinges another: How far and in what manner was contact during prayer maintained with the records of the faith, with the reading first and foremost of Sacred Scripture and also with the literature of other witnesses of Christian doctrine and life? What part did meditation on the mysteries contained in them contribute to prayer? To what extent had private prayer been formulated in word and gesture, a question which affects the liturgy to a lesser degree? In regard to vocal prayer, especially when conducted in common, the question arises whether the words used had to be composed for the occasion or whether and how far ready-made texts from the Scriptures, especially from the Psalms, had to be employed? If the latter were chosen, no little difficulty would have arisen. The text comes to us from times quite remote from ours; even when its grammatical meaning is disclosed, we still have to face an alien cultural milieu and, not the least, a pre-Christian situation. Hence ways of approach have to be sought: What were these?

A fresh question arises immediately: Wherein consists the value of prayer couched in unfamiliar if sacral terms? Was their very utterance, that is the physical effort necessary to pronounce them, regarded as an asset? Was a quantitive increase of such prayers a goal to be aimed at? Was their literally ceaseless repetition a genuine ideal, or had a personal response in and through the words to be stressed before all else, and an effort thus made to facilitate the process? How in the main was the relationship between vocal and mental prayer to be gauged?

Prayer and Life

Further: How should prayer and life be mutually related? Should prayer serve merely to find God and to solicit his help in our aspirations and needs, or conversely should it serve as a pathway to discover God's will and what he expects of us and so help us to bring our lives into harmony with it? Or should it serve at the same time as nourishment for one's spiritual life and, if need be, for one's apostolic endeavor?

Another point: What influence had all that mystique of prayer, as cultivated by the monks and clerics, on layfolk caught up in worldly affairs, on men and women who had family and society to attend to, who found it impossible to familiarize themselves with the historical milieu, say, of the Psalms, for whom in earlier days books were non-existent? What was the prayer of the ordinary, simple, people?

And last of all, had prayer an innate force capable of withstanding an enlightened age which witnessed the break-up of an order of things where each event of one's daily life seemed to be arranged and carried through by God's immediate action? Could it accommodate itself to a more sophisticated view of life in which an all-encompassing law of nature set the course of things?

All these are questions involving the history of Christian prayer during the last two thousand years. Answers to them must depend on the period with which we are dealing. They cannot be final in every case. But they do provide us with an instructive lesson today when prayer is being so sorely threatened.

1
Prayer in the Early Christian Epoch

The early Christians were conscious of the fact that they were citizens of two worlds. On the one hand they shared the civic life of their contemporaries, a point strongly emphasized on occasion by apologetic writers. Thus the author of the *Letter to Diognetus* writes:

> Christians do not form a separate group marked off from other people by land, language or customs; they do not live in towns of their own nor speak a foreign tongue nor follow a special way of life. . . . In their dress and way of living and general outward behavior they conform to native usage.

But he does not forget to add: "They take in good part all that comes their way for they are pilgrims. . . . They live on the earth but their city is in heaven."

Clement of Alexandria (died before 216 A.D.) is *the* writer of the early Christian epoch who is consciously turned toward the world; he occupied himself chiefly with the "question of living as a Christian in the world, how the Christian is to overcome the world while remaining in it." And yet prayer was a matter of such importance for him, the practice of uninterrupted prayer, that he devoted practically the whole of Book VIII of his *Stromata* to that theme. The perfect Christian, the *gnostic*, makes his whole life a prayer. What Clement primarily means is assuredly a life lived in God's presence. He is also the first writer to give us more detailed information on the daily prayer of the Christian. He mentions the custom observed by many of "fixed hours to be assigned to prayer as for example the third, the sixth and the ninth." He speaks from time to time of "canticles of praise and of Scripture readings" before meals and before retiring to rest. Prayer during the night is also mentioned and not only interior prayer but prayer also with uplifted hands and eyes directed heavenward. How highly the early Christians valued prayer is strikingly exemplified by Justin Martyr when he speaks of the Church simply as "a house of prayer and adoration as a result of Christ's cross and the water of purification."

Didache

However, we are not left to a few generalities as regards prayer in those early days. We can observe it at close quarters and learn how Christ's followers arranged their prayer-life. That they were supposed to pray three times each day is known from the *Didache* dating from the turn of the first century. And it is the Lord's Prayer that is prescribed, a ruling confirmed by Origen. Thus a fixed arrangement as regards prayer must have been the early rule and it must have been impressed on the minds of converts to Christianity, not that such a program did not admit of changes locally, nor was it ever regarded as a formal Church law. The convert naturally took it for granted that he was to adopt the Christian life-style in this matter as well as in others. From the third century onward we meet with concrete settings for this in various localities.

Tertullian

Tertullian (d. after 220) drawing obviously on his catechetical experience composed a special work "On Prayer." He subjoins to an interpretation of the Our Father an introduction to the spirit of Christian prayer; then follows with a number of practical hints like these: One's hands need not be washed every time one prays, they are already clean as the result of Baptism and so can be raised toward God, but moderately so (the deeper meaning behind the gesture is to model oneself on the crucified Lord). One need not lay aside one's mantle (paenula) while praying. It is inappropriate to sit when conversing with God in prayer. Prayer does not call for an expenditure of voice. Women and virgins should wear the veil. At the start of morning prayer at least, as well as on fast days, but not on Sundays or during Easter, one should kneel in prayer (c.23). Tertullian then offers definite suggestions as regards the hours when we should pray: They are the tertia, sexta, nona (the third, sixth and ninth hours). This, though, is not to be taken as a command but rather as a reminder to pray thrice daily, as is reported of Daniel (Dan. 6:10). These do not of course include the regular (legitimis) prayers to be said at the beginning of the day and during the night.

It is also proper for a Christian to pray before meals or before bathing: Heavenly nourishment should precede that of earth (c.25). Finally, he stresses a sense of faith and purity and the practice of good works (pompa operum bonorum: the procession of good works) which should accompany our prayer on its path to God's altar. This latter thought is a familiar one in early Christian times. For the *Pastor of Hermas* it goes without saying that prayer should be joined to fasting and almsgiving. Cyprian calls it a barren prayer (sterilis oratio) which does not go hand in hand with alms.

Hippolytus

The times given above for prayer are given form and color for the first time in the *Apostolic Tradition* of Hippolytus of Rome (around 215). A definite program for prayer is not offered, but the faithful are referred rather to the mystery of Christ and encouraged to go through the various stages in the work of the redemption each day: This can be in the form of vocal praise "when you are at home" at the third hour whereas when one is elsewhere and that time comes, one should "pray in his heart." At the third hour, also one should recall how Christ was crucified; then at the sixth hour how darkness supervened and Christ prayed on the cross with a loud voice; so too at the ninth hour it should be recalled how water and blood issued from his side and how God sent his word to the saints to enlighten them that Christ's death heralded the beginning of his resurrection.

The Christian should also pray at night before retiring and in the morning after rising, but for these times no subject-matter is mentioned. Whereas for the prayer to be said at midnight, in which his wife may join, man is to share in the song of praise intoned by creation, as at that hour the stars, the trees, the waters, angels in unison with the just, give praise to God. Or again, it was midnight when the cry rang out announcing the bridegroom's arrival. Finally, special emphasis is given by Hippolytus to a further time for prayer—before dawn "at cockcrow," when the Christian is to look out for the dawning of that everlasting light which will shine upon us with the resurrection of the dead.

This arrangement was faithfully handed on to the following centuries, as appears in a number of writings. Only Hippolytus's *Apostolic Tradition* was somewhat changed: prayer twice during the night was found to be too much of a good thing. On the other hand, one prayer-session at midnight was not considered an unreasonable demand. We must remember the long nights in those times and the conditions of lighting. The subject-matter remained substantially the same: Christ's Passion for the day prayers and for the night ones generally the Parousia, his final coming.

Times of Prayer

In the fourth century and thereafter the observance of these hours of prayer must have been a custom known throughout the entire Church and widely adhered to in practice, though chiefly as an individual effort as heretofore. In the Eastern Church the practice was strongly recommended to virgins, as is apparent from writings, among them that "On Virginity," a work long attributed to St. Athanasius. Jerome makes the same recommendation for the West, not only in his correspondence with young Roman women but also in his educational hints for Laeta, the anxious mother, whom he exhorts to accustom her little daughter Paula from an early age to rise at midnight for prayer and during the day to stay at her post at the third, sixth and ninth hours. Chrysostom makes mention of the practice in one of his sermons: If King David found time to praise God seven times a day (Ps. 118, 164), surely a Christian must find time to say his prayers at least thrice daily. Chrysostom takes it for granted that the follower of Christ prays in the morning and at night, but he demands also a session at midnight, to which even the children should grow accustomed. The intentions prayed for are the same as of old. They re-appear almost unchanged in Pseudo-Athanasius, only the resurrection is recalled, at the morning prayer. In later times, too, these themes are constantly reproduced, only they are usually made to serve as motivations for the hour in question rather than as subject-matter for the prayer. Thus in the Bobbio Missal (7th-8th century) they offer a basis for the individual canonical *Horae*. A similar function is apparent in other biblical themes which are introduced into different prayer hours: The Descent of the Holy Spirit for the third hour, Peter's prayer at the sixth hour and his entry into the Temple for the ninth, all this in accordance with an earlier tradition. Cassian introduces into the ninth hour Peter's visit to Cornelius as well. So too the hour of the Last Supper. Finally, *motivs* from the Old Testament are the slaying of the first-born in Egypt and the passage through the Red Sea.

Intentions for Prayer

Likely enough we can regard this daily programme of conversing with God as the core and kernel of Christian prayer. Not that it was confined to those central themes even in the early days of the Church. While the information we have cited stems from writings whose purpose was more or less to organize the practical prayer life of the faithful, further witnesses are available who allow us to glimpse from another angle what the prayer of the early Christians was like. In the *Pastor of Hermas* we find prayers related to the author's treatment of visions, mandates and parables, prayers for forgiveness of sin, prayers especially in which God is thanked for his benefits. "Prayer is the poor man's riches" (Sim. 2:5). The closing note in Pope Clement's letter to the church of Corinth (around the year 96) is one of praise and thanksgiving. In a comprehensive prayer the inmost soul of the writer is revealed; its range reaches to the Creator whose providence controls and orders all things and to Christ his beloved son who has chosen and sanctified us. Then follow prayers of intercession for all in distress, for the poor and the sick, for the hungry and those astray. Finally his horizon widens in a prayer that all peoples may recognize "that you alone are God and that Jesus Christ is your (divine) Son and we your people and the sheep of your fold" (c.59,4). And a renewed intercession for the leaders of the community ends in a note of praise offered to God "through the high priest and leader of our souls Jesus Christ through whom he is glorified forever" (c.62,3). In this prayer is revealed the theological structure of Christian prayer: God, the Creator and Lord of the world is its object, throned in unassailable majesty above, but he is a God too who has stooped to us in Christ. In prayer the worshiper's world of faith is necessarily mirrored with more or less clarity, but where the prayer is untrammeled and spontaneous it need not be so precise—a fully rounded, developed prayer will be the liturgical prayer which is recited by the assembled community.

Origen on Prayer

It is rather surprising that Origen in his Treatise *On Prayer* (around 233/234) requires for every prayer a rigorous systemization of this kind. He develops first the general principles affecting Christian prayer: The Holy Spirit must inspire the prayer we direct to the Father in Christ Jesus. He eulogizes the liberating power which prayer posesses, enabling us to lift ourselves from the earth Godward (c.8f.). He refers us to the Sermon on the Mount for the manner in which we should pray. The Our Father, which he expounds in detail, furnishes the intentions we are to lay before God. While stressing by various turns of expression the obligation to direct our prayer to God, to the Father, Origen adds immediately: In doing this we should not overlook the high priest whom the Father has appointed and who is the mediator of Christian prayer (c.15,4). He repeats with a certain urgency that our prayers should begin and end "with the praise and glorification of the Father through Jesus Christ in the Holy Spirit" (c.33,1; cf. c.33,3). He goes so far as to exclude prayer which is directed to Christ: "If one wishes to pray aright one must not pray to him who is himself praying . . . Whom the Father has appointed high priest and mediator" (c.16).

Here Origen betrays a lack of accuracy in his grasp of the mystery of the Trinity (he sees the mediator in the Logos); apart from this the zealousness of the great Alexandrine should be explained by the fact that his treatise was meant for this friend Ambrose, a former adherent of Gnosticism. This Christian sect, as appears from the Apocryphal Acts of the Apostles, had developed a method of prayer whereby the invisible God is no longer contacted; prayer is directed to the aeons, divine emanations, among whom Christ occupies but a pre-eminent place. On occasion Christ is even called Father; in association with him, amid other vague figures, appears his Holy Spirit, "the mother of all creation." Origen's intention here was doubtless to cure his addressee from such confusion in Christian notions. In alluding to the theory, Origen had no wish to explain the nature of Christian prayer. This is clear from the fact that he did not believe in the theory: He cites the prayer which Stephen in his death-throes addressed to Christ (c.14,6) and introduces repeatedly into his homilies, prayers similarly addressed; and in his work "Against Celsus" he cites a remark of this heathen philosopher. The latter did not take offense from the practice of the Christians in worshiping one God, but he certainly did from "the homage they pay also to this man whom they regard as the founder of their rebellion." Origen defends their position by pointing to the unity of Father and Son. Besides such behavior on the part of his followers was an obvious way of raising their minds and hearts to Christ, a spontaneous result of meditating on his mystery. The same is true of the hymns sung during religious services at all times. Of those of early date few examples have been preserved; they include the Gloria in Excelsis and the Te Deum; in the second portion of both Christ is addressed.

Spontaneous too was the prayer to Christ which fell from the lips of the Christian martyrs when they had made their life and death decision. Their brief words of prayer are reported by eye and ear witnesses, words in answer to the death sentence or appeals for courage in their agony were invariably directed to him whom they were unwilling to disown. Thus the final words of Carpus as he suffered in the flames: "Lord, you know that it is for your name that we are enduring this torment." The Abitena martyrs prayed as follows: "O Christ, the Lord, let us not be confounded. Son of God, come to our aid; help O Christ, have pity Lord Christ, give us courage to suffer." But in daily life also prayers addressed to Christ were quite a familiar occurrence as is shown in a special study of Jerome's writings (d.420). Reporting on the spiritual trials he endured in his early life as a hermit, he tells how he threw himself at the feet of Jesus bedewing them with his tears. Success in his exegetical studies was acquired only through Christ's revelation and assistance *Christo revelante, Christo adjuvante*. The verses from the Psalms in which the Lord is invoked, Jerome understands without more ado of Christ, in accordance with an interpretation already current. In early Christian times it was generally understood that the Psalms bore a meaning and an application referring to Christ. This would have arisen in two ways, either "from below" through a typological exegesis, interpreting the psalm as the voice of Christ invoking the Father in his distress, or as the voice of his Church by way of glorifying the Father, and this was the prevailing attitude in the early days and was subsequently given credence especially by St. Augustine. Or it could be "from above" by seeing Christ in the Kyrios or Lord to whom the psalmist appealed. This latter method of interpretation gained the ascendancy later, chiefly in the chanting of the liturgy.

As a last resort, a prayerful appeal to Christ is only one of the ways in which the Christian element as such is revealed in prayer. Tertullian can sum up the martyrs's prayer when he apostrophizes the heathen: "Our cry even on the rack and as the blood flows is, we honor God through Christ."

No matter what form devotion to Christ may have assumed in the early days of the faith it can be said in general that reference to the economy of salvation was kept steadily in mind. This holds not only for the classical "per Christum" which terminates the prayer; it appears also in the meditations on Christ's passion which formed the day's mental prayer. Here there was question not so much of a compassionate sharing in his physical sufferings as a contemplation of the stages in the work of our redemption of which the resurrection was a part. Thus prayer is that power which keeps alive in the Christian a consciousness of his dignity and the hope he cherishes thereby guaranteeing him moral support besides. It carries the conviction with which Hippolytus concludes his instructions on prayer: "If you perform these things and remember them and instruct one another and encourage the catechumens to do them, you will not be tempted or come to grief, since in every event you keep Christ before your eyes."

The Cross in Christian Antiquity

A confirmation of the foregoing is offered by the place which the cross occupied in early Christian practice. It is known, the cross in those days was invariably depicted without the figure of the crucified. The reason that lay behind this was not so much an aversion to showing him in his state of humilation as to bring out the richer significance hidden away in that symbol: The cross, the instrument of our redemption, had become a sign of victory, a *tropaion*, (trophy). The hymn of Venantius Fortunatus signs of the "crucis trophaeum."

The cross was closely associated with Christian piety from an early age. This is shown from the various occasions when its sign was traced on their persons by Christians, and in the areas of Syrian Christianity especially the cross was either painted on the wall of a Christian dwelling or fixed there in wood, facing Eastward, the direction which the people faced when praying. The acts of the martyr Hipparchus relate that this blood-witness of Christ paid homage to his Lord seven times daily before a cross painted on the wall of his dwelling. The custom of affixing the cross on the Eastern wall of the house can apparently be traced back to the second century. In any event it is clear that in those days both in private and at liturgical meetings worshipers faced the East when praying, the direction of the rising sun in which they discerned a symbol of the Risen Christ, the direction where they fancied lay the abode of the Blessed and from where Christ would come again and the "Sign of the Son of man in the clouds of heaven" (Mt. 24:30) would be awaited. So it can be said with truth that the cross which "lent an orientation to prayer was not merely a pointer but also a symbol of eschatological thinking in early Christianity." Thus what was later adopted in the basilicas had its origin in the homage paid to the cross in the home. The cross in the apse, shaped now to a cross of glory, gave direction also to community prayer and became the expression of Christian hope which looked upward to him who is in the glory of the Father and will one day come again. So we can rightly speak of a *stauro-centred* (cross-centered) piety of Christian antiquity. Its effect can also be discerned in early monasticism. Horsiesi, St. Pachomius' second successor in the leadership of Egyptian monasticism, describes as follows the meaning of the monastic life: "We have renounced the world and begun to follow the standard of the cross (vexillum crucis); the task of superiors, according to him is to await as leaders of their troop the arrival of the Redeemer, and to conduct a well-equipped army to him." In Syrian monasticism the writing of an ascetic, Dadisho by name, dating it is true to the seventh century, has been preserved. In it he instructs the monk to pay homage to the Holy Cross in his cell (evidently each cell had one). We have an echo of this also in the introduction to the Regula of St. Benedict: "Let us patiently share in the sufferings of Christ so that we may merit to share also in his Kingdom."

Early Monasticism

If we dwell here on the religious way of life of the oldest form of monasticism which in the fourth century (and so in the period with which we are dealing here) is mainly represented by the anchorites, a somewhat different atmosphere prevails. These early monks dwelling singly in their cells or caves far removed from human settlements purposed to practice a new form of Christian life only insofar as this was compatible with their resolve to confine to the barest minimum their relations with the world. They wished to live only for God and to enjoy as near an approach to him as was possible to mortal man here below. Consequently, their life was a life of prayer—uninterrupted prayer. This is disclosed in a special section of the *Apophthegmat* (Collections of Sayings attributed to Egyptian hermits). Epiphanius, later bishop of Salamis in Cyrpus, is assured by the monks of the monasteries he founded that they faithfully adhered to the instructions he gave, observing the third, sixth and ninth hours of prayer as well as Vespers. "And what of the other Hours," he asked, "don't you pray during them? The genuine monk must pray without ceasing or at least sing psalms in his heart."

About the middle of the fourth century, members of the Messalian sect from Syria made their appearance. True to their Manichean-dualistic principle, they wished to observe literally the rule of uninterrupted prayer. Some of them visited Lucius's hermitage and, when questioned by him about this unbroken converse with God, they had to admit that they, too, made time for meals and for sleep. They were a bit nonplussed by the hermit's further question: "And who in the meantime prays in your stead?" The hermit explained the method he himself adopted: While he is plaiting his mats he prays in his heart or in the words: "Have mercy on me, O God, as you are ever rich in mercy; in the abundance of your compassion blot out the record of my misdeeds" (Ps 50:1). From the earnings he makes from his work he deducts every day two denarii and places them at the door of his cell; the person who takes them prays for him while he eats and sleeps (n.9).

Other reports testify to the same practice of ceaseless prayer. Abba Macarius taught his disciples not to use many words when they prayed; rather they should frequently stretch out their arms saying: "Lord, as you know best and in the manner you will, have pity on me"; or when in distress: "Help me" (n.10). We have here that monologue form of prayer so highly valued in the spiritual life of later times. The great teachers of Eastern Christianity, Diadochus of Photike (5th century) and John Climacus (7th century) constantly recommended the practice. In the form of a simple repetition of the name of Jesus as the "Jesus Prayer," it has outlived the centuries.

But the *Apophthegmata* are familiar also with higher forms of prayer: They tell of abba Lot that when a monk called on him, complaining of his failure in prayer and meditation he stood up and raised his hands heavenward; suddenly his ten fingers appeared as so many flames of fire. "If you only will," he said, "you can become all afire" (n.8). It is told of abba Arsenius that on Saturday evenings he turned away from the setting sun and remained with hands raised to heaven till the rising sun shone on his face on Sunday morning (n.2). Among the Desert Fathers distinguished for their gift of prayer the most distinguished was Anthony the Hermit. The gift of mystical prayer, to which he was raised and during which he was frequently wrapt out of the senses, prepared him to become eventually the founder of Eastern monasticism. Even the struggles with the demons which Anthony had to endure (and these recur in the lives of the Desert Fathers) failed to quench his ardor for prayer. Incidentally, these hermits could offer good advice to those who pursued a simple form of prayer. John Climacus, for example, who spent many years in the desert, gave the following counsel to one who approached him: "If you find consolation or a sense of contrition in a single word of your prayer, dwell upon it, for your angel-guardian is at your side and is praying with you."

Desert Fathers

The method adopted by the Desert Fathers in regard to the externals of prayer did not lack specific forms. They prayed standing with uplifted hands facing the East. Sacred Scripture, it appears, did not occupy a prominent place in the anchorites' devotions. Many of the hermits did not have the requisite formation; for others the possession of a book seemed too expensive a luxury. It was otherwise with the consecrated virgin whom Ps-Athanasius counseled: "She should apply herself to meditation on Holy Scripture, possess a copy of the psalter and learn the psalms by heart. The rising sun must glimpse the book in her hands." These latter words passed into a proverb and reappear in the fourth century in Hippolytus' Canons: "If there is no morning meeting in the church you should take a book and read a portion of it; every morning the rising sun must find it reposing on your knees."

In coenobitic (community) monasticism conditions were different from the beginning. Scripture reading here was done in common; a single codex sufficed for all needs. In the message which Horsiesi addressed to his Pachomian community one is astonished at the wealth of biblical quotations cited. Not only that but the abbot pleads expressly for a keen interest in the Sacred Scripture on the part of the community to be shown by reading it and making themselves familiar with its contents. Athanasius testifies that Anthony the Hermit knew the Scriptures almost by heart.

Only gradually did the Book of Psalms become the Prayer and Hymn Book of the faithful and of the Church at large. In the first two centuries it was the Psalter, along with the prophetic books of Scripture, which furnished the reading matter. During that period too the Psalter gradually assumed importance in the day-to-day life of prayer. An impelling factor in promoting esteem for the Psalter was the experience gained from the way the heretics went about their work: It was by their hymns that the Manicheans had such great success in attracting recruits to their ranks. The result was a mistrust in orthodox circles for songs composed for the occasion and a preference for biblical hymns.

Sunday Service

What relationship did the practice of prayer in early Christian times as described so far, bear to the Church's public service? The personal prayers of the individual, as is evident from the foregoing, held a marked predominance at least in range. But equally evident is the fact that all prayer merged finally in the liturgy of the Church. On Sunday, the day of the week set aside for the memorial of the redemption (climaxed in the Lord's resurrection) "all those living in town or country meet in the place of assembly. In the great prayer of thanksgiving, bread and wine become the Sacrifice of Christ and of the community, as well as the Bread of Immortality" (Ignatius of Antioch). The saying attributed to the Abilena martyrs: "We cannot survive without the *Dominicum*" (the Lord's Body) can be verified in every other group of martyrs. The Mass, however, was not restricted to the Sundays. In North Africa within a small circle of worshipers it was also celebrated on working days, as we learn from Cyprian. It found its way even into the prisons where arrested Christians were detained. But this was by way of exception. The faithful were allowed to take the Blessed Sacrament home with them on Sundays, as appears from the practice in vogue in various Christian localities, in order to partake of it daily "before every other food." This privilege was a fairly regular custom of the Egyptian Fathers of the desert. The anchorites also joined the community service on Sundays (also on Saturdays as was generally customary in the East); it seemed to have been a matter of course with them, so much so that it is mentioned only incidentally in a few of our sources. Cases are reported where a priest used to come on Sundays to a recluse's hermitage in order to offer the Holy Sacrifice of the Mass. When we hear that anchorites never left their cells, this does not mean they failed to go to church on Sunday. However, there may have been at this period, as in later days, hermits who preferred to keep their undisturbed solitude on Sunday rather than visit the church as there was no formal commandment regarding Sunday observance.

2
At the Height of Christian Antiquity

After the Peace of Constantine a powerful impetus was given the Church's prayer, the Liturgy. This is observable not only in the church buildings which arose on every side but in the daily liturgical service which was celebrated in many places in addition to the Sunday eucharistic service. This was not a complete novelty; on occasions at least, as *The Apostolic Tradition* of Hippolytus testifies, at the beginning of the third century prayer meetings of the faithful were held apart from the celebration of the Eucharist. Each morning the deacons and presbyters were expected to meet the bishop and give an instruction to the people; this was in the form of a "catechesis" which closed with prayer. From time to time also the agape was held in the evenings when a well-to-do Christian invited some poorer members of the community to his home. One of the clerics had to preside at the function. The meal was preceded by a Blessing of the Light and a prayer-session at which psalms were recited and the community answered with "Alleluia."

We can recognize here without difficulty the first beginnings of the two *Horae* which in the fourth century took shape as a daily practice in the cathedral churches, namely Matins and Vespers. They are the *Horae* which from then on represent the cathedral Office as distinct from the later monastic Office and form in both the basic, irreplaceable elements of the Horae prayer. In the eighth book of the *Apostolic Constitution* (Antioch around 380) we meet with a definite ruling for the first time: The bishop is to assemble the community in the evening, the 140th Psalm (the raising of the hands "as an evening sacrifice") is recited; then follows a series of petitions read out by the deacon for individual states in life, which the bishop closes with an Oratio and his blessing. The same arrangement was observed in the morning when prayer was opened with Psalm.62, (Ad te de luce vigilo). Eusebius of Caesarea (d.339) vouches for the fact that it was a universal practice to hold morning and evening services in the churches, when hymns were sung and prayers recited. We have the same testimony for the West from Hilary of Poitiers (d.367). Somewhat later, as a matter of conscience, the observance of these two *Horae,* the *matutina et vespertina officia*, is the object of regulations of several Synods in Gaul like those of Agde (506) and Vaison (529); as also of the Synods of Braga (563) and Toledo (633 and 675) in Spain. These two *Horae* are mentioned with sufficient clarity in other places too; so, for example, for Milan by Ambrose, for North Africa by Augustine, by Paulinus for Nola. In Rome, too, these two Horae must have been in vogue, as the Sacramentaries make mention of special prayers to be said at morning and evening hours of prayer.

Church Meetings

These prayer meetings in the church were attended by the faithful, at least by those who lived in the neighborhood. Ambrose invites his hearers to come to church early in the morning when darkness prevents them from engaging in business and to start the day with hymns and songs and the "Beatitudes." The eight Beatitudes formed part, consequently, of the programme of morning prayer in Milan. Augustine tells of how his mother Monica used to come twice a day to church "in order that she might hear you in your words, and you her in her prayers." It would appear that it was preferably to Matins that the people came, doubtless for the reason given by Ambrose: Owing to lighting conditions in those days work could not begin before daylight. Cassian in conversation with abba Theonas reminds the monks of the example given by many layfolk *(saeculares)* who hurry to church before dawn (*ante lucem vel diluculo*). A similar reproach is voiced by emperor Justinian in regard to clerics of his empire: When the laity crowd the churches for the Office and show great zeal in its recitation it is unseemly for clerics to neglect a task to which they are obliged by their profession (attendance at the night Office of Matins and Vespers). Bishop Caesarius of Arles (d.540) who has the simple working people in mind in his homilies encourages his hearer to come to church before daybreak, especially during the period of the long nights, and somewhat earlier during Lent; they should take part in the Psalmody and in the prayers and attend to the readings and the bishop's sermon which was often associated with the readings. He promises to finish early "so that their time for work will not be curtailed." With equal insistence Nicetas (d. after 414) of Remesiana (a locality near the lower Danube) invites the faithful, the old and infirm excepted, to the vigils. They are asked to do this only twice in the week, on Saturday and Sunday, thus devoting *noctium portionem aliquam* (some part of the nights) to the divine service.

Elsewhere too, where we have evidence of Matins and Vespers being held, it is likely that this did not occur every day. On the other hand, the more or less regular hours for prayer led here and there to a full vigil for which the Easter Virgil served as model as early as the second century. In Rome also, such comprehensive vigils were held occasionally from Saturday to Sunday in Ember weeks. Similar prayer meetings during entire nights were not unusual especially at a martyr's grave; they could be celebrated privately for smaller groups. The Synod of Elvira (around 306) decreed that women should not take part in these assemblies (c.35); and Jerome instructed Laeta not to allow her little daughter to leave her side in the event of her attending such a vigil. That big crowds were expected to attend these morning services is evidenced from the fact that in Tours at St. Martin's grave a bell was rung to summon the faithful to Matins. At Merida in Spain too, as early as the seventh century a bell was rung for the beginning of Matins.

In time these *Horae* came to be regarded not so much as a choir prayer for clerics as a religious service for the laity, so much so that an obligation to attend had to be specially insisted upon with the former. In the churches of Gaul clerics were often allocated for service at the *Horae* according to a definite roster. Indeed, it was not unheard of that Vespers might be held without a single cleric being present.

It is clear that attendance at these daily morning and evening services was voluntary even for those who lived near the church. Though Ambrose issued repeated invitations to attend them, still he allows for prayers to be said at home instead of in the church. In any event the degree of obligation here was very different from that affecting the Sunday Mass. Attendance at the latter, following the Synod of Elvira, was formulated more and more as a Church law binding on all. Considerable allowance, however, had to be made in this matter as one had to reckon with conditions in country districts where people lived long distances from the church.

In any event, attendance at these religious services constituted an effective school of prayer for a considerable portion, indeed the backbone, of the community. They got to know the psalms well; in community services, one of the psalms was chosen which had a meaningful appeal; it was first recited by the leader who took a verse specially adapted for the purpose; this he sang once by himself to the people who repeated it as a refrain after each verse or section of the psalm. We have here the *Responsorial Type* of singing which was also used for hymn singing, as St. Ephraem's hymns testify. Such refrains with which the people became familiar were favorites with Augustine who made them the subject of his preaching thus impressing their contents the more deeply on their minds. Ambrose too has often occasion to refer to them, and Basil speaks likewise of this responsorial method of chant.

Rendering of the Psalms

The faithful were not expected to learn the psalms by heart or even a number of them. Still Chrysostom takes it for granted that every Christian was well acquainted with the morning psalm 62 and the evening one psalm 140. According to Caesarius of Arles everybody knew psalm 103 which was recited at Vespers in churches and monasteries glorifying creation, (verse 19: "the sun knows well the hour of its setting"), as well as psalm 50, the Miserere, and psalm 90 the evening prayer. In Naples, candidates for Baptism were required to know the short psalm of praise, 116, as well as learn by heart psalm 22: "The Lord is my Shepherd . . ." as a song of thanksgiving, which as newly-baptized Christians they would be singing. In this way an extensive knowledge of the Psalter was acquired, much as today the average churchgoer is familiar with a number of stanzas in the church hymns; anything beyond this can be had in printed texts. In those days the responsorial singing method supplied what was needed; the leader had the full text before him, the faithful then took over from him.

At times, however the psalms must have been sung right through (*in directum*) by the community. Indeed in Nicetas's community this seems to have been the regular way of rendering the psalms. A certain musical elaboration was also allowed for, which excluded any element of the theatrical. Nicetas is at pains to stress the *vocis consonantia,* (harmonization of voice), which must be observed when singing; there must be no dragging of the voice, no singing too high or too low on the part of an individual chorister; all should take their cue from the three young men in the fiery furnace who sang the praises of God "with one mouth." A similar method of singing was a regular feature in Basil's community, at least as far as psalm 50 was concerned around the year 375.

Just as responsorial singing familiarized the faithful with a number of verses from the Psalter, so too they learnt the various prayers from their cries of assent during divine service. In the eucharistic liturgy the ancient acclamations (to which the Sanctus was now added) were long since familiar to the people. Another addition were the answers which they gave to the litanies that were recited by the deacon. Etheria had listened with admiration to the almost endless repetition of the *Kyrie eleison* rendered by a group of children in Jerusalem. It was not long before the same invocation appeared in the West also. The Synod of Vaison (529) bears testimony to "the sweet and salutary custom of pronouncing frequently and with devotion the Kyrie eleison, a wide-spread practice which should be introduced everywhere into Matins and Vespers."

In circles which could claim a certain religious formation for their members it was understandable that prayer would be given a correspondingly suitable form borrowed evidently from the liturgy. This we observe from certain sections of Etheria's account of her pilgrimage. The authoress, who was not a nun but a directress of a loosely structured association of young women, describes the devotional exercises which she and her companions used to perform at the various pilgrim resorts in the Sinai or in Palestine. These began with a prayer which was followed by the reading of a passage from Holy Scripture treating of the locality or the event which was being commemorated. Then a suitable psalm was recited, and a prayer concluded the ceremony (c.4,3; c.10,7). Such too was the arrangement which governed divine service at that period in cathedral and community churches at Matins and Vespers, at least during full vigils, and in the service of the Word during Mass where God's Word and the hymn were followed by the prayer of the community and its church leader.

Interpreting the Psalms

The psalms undoubtedly formed the chief element in the Church's prayer. In his work on the value of the Psalmody, Nicetas of Remesiana never tires extolling the rich contents of the psalms: People of every age and class find in them food for their spiritual lives; truth, loyalty, virtue are commended, while lying and sinful conduct are stigmatized. The mystery of Christ (*Christi sacramenta*) is there the subject of the community's homage, his passion, resurrection, his place at the right hand of the Father, the inheritance of the gentiles and the outpouring of the Spirit.

As a fact, the Fathers in their exegesis of the psalms showed a tendency to interpret them in a New Testament sense. The most outstanding example of this is offered by St. Augustine's *Enarrationes in Psalmos*, fruit of his homilies to the people, in which the doctor of the Church expounds all one hundred and fifty psalms in the light of the mystery of Christ. So, too, with the headings often provided for the psalms in manuscripts dating from the sixth century in the spirit of an older tradition. In these the psalm is set in the light of salvation history and preferably designated as the *vox Christi* or *vox ecclesiae*. Similarly a large part of the Psalter-collects (the orationes) which according to custom followed on the individual psalms aimed at gathering up the Christian element which the Old Testament singer could only vaguely hint at in obscure images.

Readings also formed a certain part of the programme for both *Horae* in the early Christian services. We saw how St. Monica used to attend daily readings in church. Caesarius of Arles too not only set great store on the Matins reading in the church but also encourages the faithful to adopt the *lectio divina* in their homes. If a person enters the church while a reading is in progress, writes Nicetas of Remesiana, he should not start praying aloud himself but pay homage to the Lord (probably by a low bow), trace the sign of the cross on his forehead and attend to the reading.

What did the reading matter consist in? Sacred Scripture, obviously, in the first place. In the Eastern Church Scripture readings of normal length were customary at Vespers and Matins on Sundays and Holydays since the early Middle Ages, a practice that still obtains today. Rufinus (d. 410) speaks of "books" which were read in church, including the *Pastor Hermae*, the *Didache* and the *Judicium Petri*. Writings such as these were read at Matins but certainly not during Mass. Gregory the Great thought it his duty to object to his *Moralia in Job* being read at Matins (*publice ad vigilias*) in Ravenna as being quite unsuitable for the purpose. A story true to the life, again from the East, is recorded of Stephen the Younger (d.767), that when a boy he was often present with his mother at the vigils held at the martyrs' shrines. When the readings began he stood in front of the barrier, gazing fixedly at the reader; from the mere recital he could reproduce all that was said, whether it was an account of a martyrdom, a biography or a sermon from one of the Fathers.

We gather then that the faithful were in a position to derive spiritual refreshment of various kinds from the public services they attended. Yet subsequent to the fifth century mention of Christ's passion is strikingly absent from daily prayer. Not that remembrance of it was totally dropped, as will appear at a later period. Even the observance of the daily *Horae* remained an ideal; but its reality in terms of prayer passed to the monasteries; only a few lay worshipers would have joined in the monks' devotions.

Daily Prayers

The daily prayers said by the faithful in their homes were the morning and evening ones. That every Christian was bound to say them in some form or another we learn from certain reminders, chiefly concerning the Pater Noster and the Creed. A fragment from a writing of Nicetas of Remesiana is preserved in which he mentions the catechesis for candidates for Baptism: the catechumens are to be trained "to retain in memory the Symbolum (Creed) and say it daily before going to sleep and on rising. So too with the Lord's Prayer and the sign of the Cross with which each arms himself against the devil." The same instruction recurs in St. Augustine's catechesis in regard to the Our Father and the Creed. He is chiefly concerned that these formulae which had been given only orally should be firmly fixed in memory, evidently for the purpose of providing a strengthening food for the mind. Ps-Ambrose advises virgins to go to sleep with the Lord's Prayer on their lips and say it again on rising and to recite the Creed daily in the early morning hours. That these two venerable formularies should be reckoned as firm supports of the spiritual life of all Christians is testified by Caesarius of Arles when he advises his faithful: "Whenever you have to go anywhere, sign yourselves with the Name of Jesus Christ, say the Symbolum (the Confession of Faith) or the Lord's Prayer and go your ways sure of the divine protection." This advice is repeated in the following centuries under the definite prescription to recite both sacred texts at least twice daily, morning and evening. The instruction thus given the neophytes became a rule of life; it was observed as a matter of course by monks and clerics as appears from the canonical hours in which the Our Father and the Symbolum spoken in a subdued voice formed the beginning of prayer in the morning and at the day's close in the evening. It continued to be observed for over a thousand years until, in the Reform of the Rubrics in 1955, it was omitted, doubtless without reflecting on the origin and antecedents of the custom.

St. Augustine on Prayer

Though our information regarding prayer said privately in the home is scanty enough at this period, there remains the fact that there was no lack of encouragement for Christians to engage in fervent prayer nor of instruction on how to pray properly. St. Augustine has left us an important treatise on prayer which he dedicated to Proba, a rich widow, in answer to a request of hers; apparently it was meant for domestic use by her and her lady friends (n.30). To pray, he says, is to yearn for the *vita beata* (the blessed life) in faith, hope and love and this is to be found only in the *vita aeterna* (eternal life). And to that extent prayer must be an abiding state of the Christian, as appears from the commandment to pray always. But to prevent this yearning from being extinguished, we must also at certain times turn the mind to prayer and with the words of the prayer remind ourselves of our duty. In this way we remain receptive of what God wills to grant us. Prayer that lasts for a long time is also praiseworthy provided our duties allow us the time. We do not, however, need to make many words of it. Augustine is familiar with and approves of the practice of the "Egyptians" and how they make use of "very brief, quickly despatched prayers" (orationes brevissimas et raptim quodammodo jaculatas). In particular, the Our Father contains all that we should pray for. Besides, according to the words of the Apostle we are ignorant of what we should ask (Rom. 8:25f.); in which connection Augustine speaks of a *docta ignorantia* (a learned ignorance), (n.28). On other occasions he treats expressly of the prayer of petition; we should not unconditionally ask for earthly favors; we can be sure of being heard only if we pray "In the Name of Jesus," that is when we desire what serves our spiritual welfare, and even then we can expect a favorable answer only for ourselves. To conclude, Augustine stands out himself as a man of intense prayer: His *Confessions* constitute one unique prayer, as humble as it is heartfelt. Caesarius of Arles, the popular preacher, does not gainsay the great doctor of the Church but he is more broadminded where temporal favors form the subject of prayer: provided they are not what is chiefly desired, we should desire before all else the soul's well-being and eternal life for ouselves and all others. A pre-condition that God will hearken to our prayer is that we have been hearkening to him before we pray; also that all rancor must be banished from the heart. Caesarius's attention is focussed rather on the external posture adopted at prayer. In the church one should pray silently and not disturb one's neighbor. One should imitate the example of Anna in the first Book of Kings who only moved her lips (1 Kg 1;10,13). During prayer the mind should not turn to other things. He devotes a whole homily to explaining to his hearers how they should behave when the deacon calls the *Flectamus genua* or when he invites them to bend the knee before the bishop gives his blessing. The publican, not the Pharisee, in the temple should be their model; he who will drink from the spiritual well which is Christ and from the torrent of the Holy Spirit must do so in a bending posture.

3
In the Monasteries of the Early Middle Ages

Thus far we have had the Christian people in mind and their large-scale involvement in the two *Horae*, Matins and Vespers. What of the remaining hours of daily prayer? Here we encroach on the domain of rising monasticism; not that we are without trace of lay participation in these extra prayer hours. In addition to a private recitation of Terce, Sext and None, Chrysostom is aware of a public celebration of them in church. He makes a serious effort, attended with but moderate success, to interest the faithful in coming to church for night prayer as well as for morning devotions. In the *Testamentum Domini* mention is made of a prayer of a solemn character held at a very early hour in the church for Terce and Sext. This was in addition to a community prayer at midnight which the *sacerdotes et perfectiores* (priests and more perfect souls) attended. Caesarius of Arles encouraged his people to come to church during Lent, not only for Matins but also for Terce, Sext and None.

Something similar is contained in the report left to us (c. 400) by the Western pilgrim Etheria with reference to the service celebrated daily in Jerusalem. Here both *Horae* at morning and evening were well attended. They were clearly distinct from a prayer meeting at night, at cockcrow, which preceded the public morning hour and from the prayer hours at Sext and None (only in Lent was Terce usual). These meetings were attended mostly by consecrated virgins and by monks, the Monazontes (Solitaries) who had come to this pilgrim center. We have to do here with groups of ascetics in their transitional stage from anchorite to monk. What the pilgrim reports on the psalmody of these hours of prayer is significant enough. Prayer followed on the various sections of the Psalter and for this two or three priests or deacons stood ready as a rule to lead the prayer (c.24,1). We have here an effort to get the Church's seal of approval for these semi-private groups and lend them the dignity of a church liturgy. It is abundantly clear that in these ascetical groups can be recognized the first stages on the road leading to genuine monasticism and in their prayer the first beginnings of a fully monastic Office.

Basilica-Monasteries

Besides Jerusalem there were other sanctuaries where zealous Christians assembled who wished to lead a more intensive religious life, chiefly at martyrs' graves, but also at cathedral and community churches. They joined in the usual divine service, rounding it off by further hours of prayer, in this falling in line more or less with existing tradition. Bishops in various localities backed up the efforts of these *devoti*, since in that way the praises of God in their basilicas went on uninterruptedly day and night. A section of these devout people would settle down in the neighborhood of the sanctuary and finally adopt a common way of life. In this manner arose what were called basilica-monasteries. We can conclude to a foundation of the sort from what Basil (d.379) reports of his church in Caesarea. At Rome the first foundations of this kind are attested to in the middle of the fifth century; they grew rapidly in number and importance; in the eighth century there were sixty of these basilica-monasteries in the Eternal City. Clerics who may have taken part in the services of these basilica-monasteries may be regarded as forerunners of the later canons of cathedral and collegiate chapters, whose constitution set up after the year 816 is clearly distinguished from that of the monks. It is a known fact that they enjoyed high favor in Rome with many popes: Gregory the Great handed over to their charge the entire pastoral care of San Pancrazio, replacing secular priests who had failed to measure up to their task.

Here was developed what we know in the Roman Liturgy as the *officium divinum*, the fully organized cursus of the canonical hours, each made up of psalms, and concluding with a church prayer. The three day-hours and a night hour with a Nocturn or Nocturns are added to the two hours of the cathedral arrangement and further increased (first in the monasteries proper) by Prime and Compline. The "seven times daily praises" (ps. 118, 164) which since Clement of Alexandria's day were in their broader sense constantly cited as an ideal for prayer were now literally fulfilled in seven church hours of prayer. As the night Horae could be regarded as forming a unit with Matins (Lauds)—from the later Middle Ages onward it had not only taken over from the latter the name *Matutinum* but was generally regarded also as a mere extension of Matins—the Office had now seven not eight Horae.

Roman Office Readings

That it was the basilica-monasteries of the kind mentioned which played a special part in initiating the traditional Roman Office is confirmed by the structure of the individual Horae. Apart from the Nocturns of the night Horae they all display in the earliest sources, including St. Benedict's *Regula*, a characteristic feature. This is the peculiar division into two sections: We have first a psalmody consisting of three or five psalms and then a prayer arrangement like the one which Etheria witnessed and which is in keeping with the elements of a somewhat formal community service made up respectively of readings, hymn and prayer (in the language of today's Breviary, Capitulum, Responsorium and Oratio).

It is now certain that readings were, generally speaking, foreign to the Office of earlier oriental monasticism as well as to the people's Day Hours in the East. The Horae consisted in the main of psalmody and the relevant Oratio. Only on Sundays and feast days, on occasions namely when the entire community was expected to be present was it early the custom, in the Syrian rite, and later in the Byzantine rite, to insert readings into the people's Horae; these have been maintained to the present, as we have already seen. It was, however, the monks of the Pachomian monasteries in Egypt who led the way as early as the fourth century in appending readings to the long succession of psalms in the Office. These readings were little more than loosely connected sequences, but they served nevertheless in the West also as a stimulus to add brief readings to the psalmody, including now all the Horae. These readings, however, were of a semi-private character. It is significant that they were not retained when the Pachomian order of things was adopted by the Syrian monasteries.

The *Regula Benedicti* had taken the same step as regards the inclusion of Readings in its Divine Office. But all points to the fact that it was not Benedict who first introduced them; their origin lay in one of the Roman city basilica-monasteries whose occupants were wont to take part, along with the layfolk and the clergy in the recitation of the old cathedral Horae, and then out of personal devotion added the further Horae, retaining the same structure for them.

We can affirm then with assurance that the ascetics of the basilica-monasteries remained not only spatially in the neighborhood of the city and its churches; they represented also in their prayer-life an intermediate and adjusting stage between the services of the cathedral and parish churches and the prayer-pattern of pure, primitive monasticism whose inheritance they had taken over in other respects as well. In their converse with God not only was room and scope left for Eucharist and liturgy in the old sense, but Eucharist and Liturgy were unequivocally the pivotal points of their religious programme. It will be useful then to examine more closely the inheritance they brought with them to the sanctuary: the prayer cult of a monasticism which had chosen as its basic principle world-remoteness and desert, a way of life in which Eucharist and Liturgy were present indeed but very definitely relegated to the background.

Monasticism such as this was familiar with community prayer. The anchorites' experience went to show fairly soon that the life of a hermit, left to his own devices, presupposed a spiritual maturity of a high order and that living in common with others had definitely to be the usual approach even for Godseekers. Basil the Great opted decisively for this view. The future lay then with the monasteries that catered for the coenobitic way of life in the East and with more reason in the West. Community prayer had played an important role from the beginning in monastic community living; community prayer is vocal prayer. Now unbroken prayer, which could not be performed in a few hours, was the precious tradition inherited from the earliest days of monasticism. How could that inherited ideal be combined with the claims of a life lived in community?

Cassian on Monastic Prayer

The monks' attitude to prayer we can best learn from John Cassian who around 420 in his *Institutiones* treats exhaustively of the way prayer was organized in the monasteries and equally in detail of continual prayer and its conditions in his *Collationes* (Conferences). Before founding the famous monastery of St. Victor in Marseilles he had visited Egypt about the year 385. There he spent over a decade with the Fathers of the Nitria and Skete deserts, and in his many conversations with them he acquired spiritual experiences of various kinds. There too he had made his own a theory of the spiritual life proposed by a highly educated monk who had lived in the Nitria desert and who was re-discovered only in our century, Evagrius Pontikus (d.399). Hence Cassian's doctrine reproduces "the experience of anchorite monasticism formulated within the framework of the theology of Evagrius." In his conversation with the monk Isaac, Cassian develops his doctrine on prayer. Prayer is the proper task of the monk; successful prayer presupposes the sedation of all one's passions, the renouncing of all worldy interests. Basically there are as many types of prayer as there are different persons praying, nay as many as there are different states of mind (Coll. IX,8). The kinds of prayer which St. Paul mentions in passing (1 Tim. 2:1) Cassian tries to marshal in ascending order: With Evagrius he starts the ascent with the petitioning of God's pardon (*obsecratio*); then follows a turning away from the world (*oratio*), then prayer for the welfare of others (*postulatio*), then the prayer of thanks (*gratiarum actio*), which Cassian stresses as the noblest type of prayer. He shows from an exposé of the Our Father (VIII, 18-24) that all the intentions for which we should pray are contained in it. It marks the summit we should reach in our ascent to God; it represents that stage in the soul's progress where contemplative prayer is directed to God alone and the fire of love is enkindled as we speak with God our Father (IX,18-25). We must bend all our efforts to achieve that *jugis oratio*, continuous prayer, which allows us to share in the blessed life of the angels, the ideal *vita angelica* so frequently extolled in later times. A help toward this goal (and here abba Isaac is apparently betraying a closely guarded secret of the anchorites) is the ceaseless repetition of the single verse "Come to my aid, God; Lord, make haste to help me." These words are to be repeated on every occasion, day and night, as a defense against the eight capital vices, as also in times of consolation and desolation (X,10). By constantly confessing oneself to be God's beggar one attains to the first of the Beatitudes, poverty of spirit (X,11). The psalms will then no longer be regarded as words of the prophetic singer but be interpreted with deep emotion of heart (compunctio) as the expression of one's own chequered life. Finally, prayer will reach that perfect stage when it can dispense with words or images and pour itself out before God in inexpressible sighs (X,11).

In another passage Cassian follows his master Evagrius and the latter's Alexandrian gnosis when he distinguishes three stages in the ascent of prayer. The first is the contemplation of God's revelation in creatures; then follows the mystery of the Incarnation where the divine blends with the earthly and something of the "*judaica infirmitas*" (Jewish disability) still obtrudes. The final state is reached in the contemplation even here below of the One and the Eternal. Cassian, however, is at pains in insisting that the goal to which all prayer must be directed is love.

No doubt such a concept of prayer represents a lofty idealism, a soaring to heights which can only be glimpsed with a sense of awe and wonderment. Still it must be said of this doctrine on prayer what Olphe-Gaillard has established with reference to Cassian's spiritual teaching as a whole: It is characterized by a twofold element: an "intellectualist mysticism and an essentially monastic doctrine of perfection." Isolation from the world is brought almost to the verge of a negation of the world; scarcely a glance is vouchsafed even for Christ; Church and Sacrament are airily bypassed; life hereafter is anticipated in a manner that can be allowed only to the few who point beyond things of earth as a sign for others. However, Cassian exerted a powerful influence on later generations, not so much through his theory of the spiritual life (if we except some individual elements like his doctrine of the capital sins) as from what he reports in his *Institutiones* in praise of the coenobitical life as it was lived in the monasteries of the East. This is particularly true of the organization of their community prayer.

In this connection, it was generally taken for granted that prayer in common meant the rendering of the Psalmody in common. Caesarius of Arles, also, for example, when composing an Office arrangement for his sister's convent sums up his work as an Instruction on "how you ought to recite the psalms" (quomodo psallere debeatis). Cassian is acquainted with a more ancient tradition of Egyptian monasticism in which great latitude still prevailed and a choice was left the monks in various monasteries to recite during the night session twenty or thirty or more psalms. This was in addition to those said at the three Day-Hours, each of which consisted of six psalms. This is in line with the rule laid down by Ps-Athanasius for the night office of a virgin (and evidently for that of nuns' convents as well): "recite as many psalms as you can recite standing." In Egypt, as Cassian reports, the council of the elders prescribed the norm to be followed: twelve psalms for an evening Office and the same number for a night Office. The presumption was that during the day each monk arranged in his own way for prayer and words of Scripture to accompany his manual work (Inst. III,2).

In the *Consultationes Zachaei et Apollonii* dated about 412 and roughly contemporaneous with Cassian, we read of various degrees in monastic life differentiated according to the fervor with which the monks recited the Psalter. Lowerst in rank were those who manifested no particular zest for their task (psallendi vigore non fervent): next to them were monks who were intent on variety in their recital (psallendi vero intentis crebra sunt studia). The most fervent were those who, when on occasion they interrupted their continual prayer, sang God's praises in the psalms (psallendi gratia). It thus appears that the rendering of the psalms was an external activity that did not count as one's real prayer. This seems true enough, as in the monastic arrangement for the Office it was a rule from the beginning to take the psalms simply in the order of the biblical Psalter, one after the other without regard to theme or connection, merely as sacral words proceeding from the mouth of God and returning to God, as though the sole purpose in view were the words themselves and a desire to find one's repose in them and thus to draw near to God.

This explanation seems to be the correct one as we come across arrangements of the Office which aimed at the greatest possible quantitative measure in reciting the psalms. A Coptic *Rule of the Synaxis*, in connection with traditions traceable to Pachomius, mentions an instruction whereby sixty psalms had to be recited during the day and fifty during the night. St. Benedict recalls that Fathers before his time had performed the entire Psalter in a single day, a feat which he would have distributed among the days of one week. Somewhat later the Rule of St. Columbanus demands along with the normal task of the day's psalms an amount of prayer for the night Office which, depending on the length of the nights, numbered thirty-six psalms and in the nights of Saturday and Sunday could increase to seventy-five psalms. Several rules for Irish monks prescribed without qualms the daily performance of the "*three fifties*," that is the entire Psalter. Elsewhere on various occasions the same was demanded at full vigils. On Good Friday in many monasteries during the High Middle Ages it was usual to go through the whole Psalter, not so much out of a dcsirc to reach an impressive total as to meet the necessity of filling out a definite period of time in a suitable manner.

Laus Perennis

Zeal in the recital of the Office led a step further in many monasteries where the monks set themselves the task of spending a day and a night in uninterrupted praise of God. This was the case with those Greek monks of the fifth century to whom the people soon gave the name of the *Non-Sleepers* (Akiometes) though the Psalter does not appear at least in the beginning to have been the chief subject of their devotions. After their founder's death they carried on their task, but in a more mitigated form: by dividing themselves into three groups (normae) each of which was responsible for eight hours of service.

A little later the movement of the *laus perennis* (the continuous praise of God) is found also in the West. Its origin is traced to the Agaunum-St. Maurice monastery founded in the year 515. The charter of its foundation prescribed that the Psalter should be recited day and night without interruption. This was secured by a division of the monks into five *normae*, each relieving the other in turn while retaining the usual basic day and night Horae. To enable the monks to carry on their task without material worries the monastery was richly endowed by King Sigismund of Burgundy, its founder, "for the salvation of my (pro animae meae salute)," as it was worded in the charter of foundation and "in the expectation that the monks with all the greater devotion would petition God's mercy for us (pro nobis Dei misericordiam). The movement was joined by a number of Gallican monasteries like the Centula (St. Riquier) in the ninth century. Given such an esteem for the Psalmody, it is not surprising that stress was laid on knowing the psalms by heart; in the Rule of Ferreolus (d.581) this is expressly prescribed.

Psalm and Genuflection

We may ask how the psalmody was arranged before it took the shape in which we find it in the Rule of St. Benedict and in the kindred system of the Roman basilicas, a shape which has been retained down to our day. Apart from the cathedral Horae and Compline it simply followed the biblical psalter *currente psalterio*, as was fundamental even in the Roman-Benedictine arrangement. The desire was merely to enter God's presence in a prayerful mood and to linger there. But this approach was taken quite seriously, as we gather from Cassian in particular. In Egypt, of the twelve psalms of the Horae, eleven were so arranged that one of the monks sang a psalm while the others listened sitting; at the conclusion of each psalm all rose and prayed in silence with arms outstretched and then knelt for a moment. The presiding monk then pronounced the Oratio each time. The twelfth psalm was an "Alleluia" one whose verses were answered with "Alleluia," in a responsorial manner, in that mode of delivery which was to be more strongly emphasized in the monastic rules of the West during the sixth century. The silent standing for prayer most likely had the purpose of allowing the psalm to linger in the mind; being prayer and an encounter with God one had to stand, as ancient custom prescribed. Then followed the genuflection, an expression obviously of adoring homage. It is significant that this bending of the knee as an element of prayer is attested to in various localities even before Cassian's day. As a prelude to the Oratio and in answer to the Summons *Flectamus genua* it constitutes one of the most ancient traditions of the Roman liturgy. St. Basil speaks of psalmody and genuflection in the same breath, regarding both as correlated requirements even for private prayer. The Ps-Anthanasius demands a genuflection after each psalm. The founder of the *Akoimetes* expects his monks to accompany the Gloria call of the angels with a genuflection seven times seventy each day.

But it is in later days especially that psalm and genuflection are combined. Isidore of Seville is aware of the connection. St. Columbanus (d.615) in his *Regula Coenobialis* prescribes that after each psalm all are to put themselves on their knees and remain in that posture while they recite three times the *Deus in adjutorium meum intende, Domine ad adjuvandum me festina* (Incline to my aid, God, Lord, make haste to help me). The same rule recurs in the Constitutions for

Irish religious bodies. These frequent genuflections were one of the peculiarities which struck people when Irish missionaries appeared on the continent. A *Life* of St. Patrick from the eighth century mentions his custom of rising each night to recite one hundred psalms which were accompanied by two hundred genuflections. As a fact, not merely Irish legends but the Rules for Irish religious associations also attest to a similar ratio, two genuflections to one psalm. However, the arrangement whereby each psalm was followed by a single geunflection prevailed. This bending of the knee was subsequently given a new significance when it became an important element in Irish penitential practice: In certain cases the recitation of some thirty psalms with as many genuflections was imposed as a penance. Even obligations to fast could be fulfilled by saying an appropriate number of psalms, each accompanied by a genuflection.

Psalter Collects

A feeling for hierarchical order is apparent from the fact that the pause for silent prayer after each psalm is terminated by the Oratio of the presiding monk. He is said to gather up the prayer, *precem colligit*, a fairly widespread regulation which was also observed in organizing prayer in the monasteries. Toward the end of Christian antiquity we also find formal compilations of *Psalter-Collects*, closing prayers for each individual psalm in which its leading thought, frequently interpreted in a Christian sense, is taken up and developed prayerfully. An effort is here discernible to penetrate the content of the prayer-text and lend it at the same time a Christian overtone. This applied even when the Psalter was worked through in sequence, one psalm following on another. A similar effort is even more clearly apparent in the case of *Psalm-Headings* of which six series for each of the one hundred and fifty psalms are still extant. They were drawn up between the sixth and eighth centuries and further transmitted in special lists reaching to the High Middle Ages. A Christian significance by way of typological fulfillment was given each psalm: The psalm is either the voice of Christ or the voice of the Church praising God's grandeur or invoking his help. Another method of imparting a Christian character to the psalms was the custom of adding a New Testament doxology, the *Gloria Patri*, to each of them, in which all present were supposed to join. Though practiced in the West in Cassian's time he found no trace of it in the East (Inst. II,8).

The Office arrangement, as reported by Cassian for the East, in what regards the treatment of the individual psalm surprisingly is found again in the much-discussed *Regula Magistri*. Whatever verdict is reached in the big controversy touching the relation of dependence between it and the Benedictine Rule, the *Regula Magistri* represents, in the matter under review, an earlier tradition which was abandoned by Benedict. Apart from some exceptions each psalm ends with the *Gloria Patri*, but then there follows a silent prayer with genuflection and the *rogus Dei* (rogus, rogatio, oratio) by which was meant a litany-patterned Oratio. Also in the prayer-arrangement with which we are familiar in the Gallic centers of the early sixth century the psalmody (whether the single psalm is meant remains uncertain) is followed by silent prayer with genuflection and then the Oratio.

Benedict's Office

Benedict's arrangement, or rather that of a Roman basilica-monastery which he follows, retains the Gloria Patri for the individual psalms. These latter then appear to follow one another without a closure; only at the end of the Horae instead of the genuflection and pause for prayer we have a short Kyrie-Litany and the Oratio in which the Pater Noster usually figures. The tension created between a working-through the Psalter *currente psalterio*, dispensing with any selection of psalms, and prayer of a genuine type must have been felt by Benedict: At any rate he selects his psalms for Matins and Compline. But the selection he adopts has reference no longer to scenes from the passion. While adhering in the morning Office to the usual psalms that acted as its framework, account is taken of the dawning light and at evening of night repose which recurs when darkness supervenes. In this he is evidently borrowing from a tenet fundamental to the cathedral order of prayer. For the rest he is content to reduce the volume of prayer by distributing over a period of one week the remaining "antiphonal" psalms of the Psalter and by shortening the Responsorial Psalms (which in the *Magister* represented full-length psalms) giving them the Responsorium form which they have retained to the present and arranging for their insertion into the lessons. In both these measures Benedict may likewise have had previous models before him. In allocating prayers to the individual Horae regard had always to be had to the day's sacral character; this was now brought into greater relief by a hymn adapted to the Hora in question (c.17). In the nineteenth chapter of his Rule entitled *De Disciplina Psallendi* Bernard recalls that it is in God's presence and *in conspectu angelorum* (in the angels' sight) that a proper recital of the Office takes place (Ps. 137,1); consequently in the oft-quoted phrase it should be said in such a manner that *mens concordet voci* (mind and word harmonize). Finally, a decisive guarantee of success in praying the psalms lies in what ancient Benedictine tradition prescribes, and what Cassian had already stressed (Coll. IX,26), namely in a clear and dignified recital which of itself is calculated to enkindle the "fervor" of genuine prayer.

Prayer and Work

However much the psalmody lent a distinctive character to corporate worship in coenobitic monasteries and indeed formed, it would appear, the actual content of the monks' converse with God, it would be a mistake to regard them as identical. Benedict made definite allowance for personal individual prayer (c.20,52). The lofty ideal of ceaseless prayer which the Desert Fathers realized after their own fashion was also held in high esteem in the monasteries of the West; only it assumes another form. The almost impossible task, psychologically speaking, of combining with serious work an attitude of unbroken prayer, or of accompanying it with prayerful words, was not demanded. In the Benedictine ideal of *Ora et Labora* (Pray and Work) work means a serious rationalized achievement, capable of guaranteeing a good economic status for a fairly large community. There is a clear distinction between it and prayer. But the *Ora* reaches far beyond the choir hours of prayer; it occupies all the time that is not claimed for work. This is clearly indicated by Rule 48: In order that idleness may have no place in the house "the brothers should be occupied at definite times with manual labor and at definite times with meditated reading (lectio divina)." In addition to the Office in choir the same emphasis is laid on *lectio divina* as on work. In the *Carta Caritatis*, a later version of the Benedictine rule drawn up by the Cistercians, the Order's programme is summarized in three points: *opus Dei* (or Office), *lectio divina*, and *labor manuum*. In addition to a general statement regarding this meditated form of reading the Benedictine rule assigns a generous measure of time to it: In summer, following on three hours of manual work, two hours of reading each morning before the midday meal.

Jerome and the Lectio Divina

The great theoretician and champion at once of the *lectio divina* was St. Jerome. His whole life's work was under its spell. Scripture reading meant for him and for his pupils of both sexes a study of the Bible beginning with the languages involved and an enquiry into the literal meaning of the sacred word. It meant also a prayerful penetration into its more profound allegorical content. This latter was the goal in view. Jerome speaks enthusiastically of the heavenly nourishment it offers. A favorite conception of his was the *Table of the Word* standing side by side with the *Table of the Sacrament*, a conception given currency in the Second Vatican Council. Fully in keeping with this view Scripture reading as another form of prayer is mentioned in the same context as the latter. Actually this was no novel idea. Cyprian shortly after his conversion writes to his friend Donatus in these terms: "Prayer or reading should be your constant concern; you speak with God and God then speaks with you." Scripture reading in their cells was a well-known practice with the Desert Fathers. Significant was the resolve of that monk who, possessing no Holy Scripture of his own, served for quite a time as farm-hand in order to purchase a codex from his earnings. It seems to have been a rule that each monk, should possess a codex containing at least some portions of the Bible. But this would have to be supplemented by other parts which he would have to learn by heart. In St. Pachomius' monasteries, when an unlearned person appeared at the gate and asked for admittance, one of the first things to be demanded of him was that he learn twenty psalms, two letters of the apostle or a similarly equivalent part of the Scriptures. He had then to learn how to read. In the *Regula Magistri* a suggestion is frequently made to "meditate or impress on the memory" something from the Scriptures—this preferably after the Nocturns, and in winter during the interval between the day hours. For this purpose groups of ten should sit together and listen to the reader. In summer this should be done in the evenings after Vespers.

A scarcity of books as well as their cost was evidently a compelling reason why considerable portions of the readings were soon relegated to the Office programme. Cassian, as we have seen, was aware of this. In Egyptian monasteries the reading took place after the evening and night Offices; elsewhere community reading followed on Vespers. In the Benedictine rule, as also in that of the *Magister*, it was prescribed that lengthy readings should be allotted to the night Hours, whereas each of the other Hours should also have its own reading. This, however, should be gone through *ex corde* (from the heart) drawing on the abundant material which the monks had memorized and had made their own—all this, however, without prejudice to the time already mentioned for personal *lectio divina*.

In view of these antecedents of the monastic Office readings it is understandable that when necessary these could be curtailed at will. Regard for the hour of the day demanded that Matins should begin as soon as daybreak set in. At that moment the reading could be interrupted once the singing of the prescribed psalms was concluded. For a similar reason in monasteries of the Middle Ages, in which long since an extensive programme had been added to Scripture reading in the shape of legends of the saints, martyrologies and collections of homilies, a good portion of these readings was as a rule transferred to the community refectory.

In general terms it must be stated that if for learned circles, especially in later times, the *lectio divina* meant chiefly a scientific preoccupation with Scripture, its purpose for the average monastery dweller and many far beyond its borders was to serve simply as spiritual reading, that meditative sort which reflected on and savored Scripture and which in later times was called meditation and interior prayer. As shown by St. Caesarius especially, this turning to account of God's word for the benefit of the monks was not confined to them alone: in his sermons to the people he encourages them not only to listen to it in the church but to read it themselves in their homes or get it read, and when necessary, to pay someone to read it for them.

4
Piety in the Carolingian Age

In tracing the period of transition to the Carolingian epoch we are confronted first with the world of Irish-Scottish Christianity. In the religious development of the West in the early Middle Ages Ireland played a decisive role. Here too it is with monastic piety only that traditional sources make us acquainted. But the representatives of this monasticism, unlike those of oriental and much less continental monasticism, far from living a life of isolation from the people imprinted a stamp of their own on the spiritual outlook of an entire nation. The career of Ireland's national apostle St. Patrick (d.461) may have been a pointer to the origins of this special type of spirituality. After spending part of his early life as a slave in a still pagan Ireland he received his decisive formation on the continent, where he also became acquainted with the monastic life.

Considerable source-material is available in helping us reach a closer knowledge of prayer as practiced in the Island of Saints. In addition, a good deal of research based on a mass of Irish sources has been undertaken. From these we learn that in Irish monastic life too the Office played a central part. St. Columbans' arrangement of it, as shown above, pointed definitely to an Egyptian tradition which would have come to Ireland by way of Lerins and Arles. It had provided for quite a considerable amount of prayer. But in Ireland we have the phenomenon of an extra burden in the shape of private prayer to be undertaken by the individual monk, a burden which far outweighed what he was already expected to perform. Once more it is the Psalter which is given pride of place. Lives of saintly men tell of monks who in addition to the Office recited the entire Psalter every day; and according to certain texts this was actually a matter of rule in some places. The Psalter was divided into *three fifties*. Each of these, according to the *Rule of Tallaght* (9th century) was subdivided into four sections; at the end of each section a genuflection followed with a Deus in adjutorium (To my aid, O God); on the conclusion of the series of fifties three Cantica were added.

Lorica Prayer

In addition to the psalms an abundant supply of hymns and of rhymed prayers in particular were available. These offered the advantage of expressing more clearly the Christian content of the prayers. Metrical structures and in later days the rhyme (both of which were employed even for the closing Oratio) were evidently meant as aids to memory. A favorite type of prayer was the so called *Borica* or Breastplate, a formulary in Latin or Celtic and arranged in a litany pattern. A large number of Irish prayers were structured in that manner. They invoked the protection of the heavenly powers, beginning with the three Divine Persons and descending from the angels to the saints of one's own nation. Long lists of threatened points of attack were drawn up, bodily organs chiefly, for which help and protection against demonic powers were solicited. Not infrequently the word Lorica was employed to express this protection, for instance a prayer of this type reads: "Gabriel, esto mihi lorica; Michael, esto mihi balteus; Raphael, esto mihi scutum (Be my breastplate; be my belt; be my shield). Christ himself is designated as Lorica. There is practically no Lorica mentioned that does not include long series of saints' names; occasionally a whole calendar of them is mounted. Prayers to individual angels and saints occupy a large space in the Book of Cerne. Events in salvation history are also invoked for protection: Thus in the Celtic Breastplate of Patrick; "I bind to myself today the power of Christ and his baptism, the power of his cross and burial, the power of his resurrection and ascension into heaven, the power of his coming on judgment day." A good deal of emphasis is laid on bodily gestures in prayer. We have already mentioned the genuflections of the Irish. The tracing of the sign of the cross on the forehead was also constantly associated with prayer. A favorite practice of Irish penitential piety was the *Crossfigell* (crucis vigilia) namely persevering in prayer with arms outstretched for as long as possible. Psalm 118 could be recited with one hundred accompanying genuflections or in crossfigell.

Irish Piety

These few indications give us an idea of the new type of prayer that was emerging, a type not found elsewhere (if at all) with such distinctness. Apart from the Office, vocal prayer was also emphasized though not to such a degree as to exclude the claims of devotion. But this vocal prayer aimed not so much at detachment from the world in order to seek repose in God alone: It was viewed rather as an achievement, the performance of a task to which one was obliged or which one had undertaken voluntarily. And this task could reach a scale in Irish monasteries which approximated to a *laus perennis*, but a *laus perennis* undertaken by the individual monk and not by the collective community. When the mystery of redemption was treated and a commanding role assigned to the cross, redemption and cross were considered as protecting powers rather than subjects for meditation. The gospel message was announced but in a manner that did not really satisfy the heart. Striking, too, is the shift of emphasis to the Divinity in Christ and to the Blessed Trinity, a resurgence of theological formularies dating from the time of the christological struggles. Of spiritual readings there is hardly a mention. One seeks protection from dangers threatening body and soul from all sides. The Christian drive toward prayer is powerfully stimulated by a fear of demons, an inheritance probably from a paganism which was never fully overcome. Added to this was a consciousness of sin which was never completely aware of the victorious redemption achieved through Christ. This phenomenon runs through practically all prayer and finds in the various *apologias* (formulas of self-accusation) an almost unnerving expression.

Thus Irish spirituality appears as a blend of "ancient church tradition with Spanish-Gallic Anti-Arianism and a Celtic religiosity which was still strongly stamped by paganism," (W. Godel) a deduction which merits further investigation. Nevertheless, the spirit of Irish faith succeeded in the seventh and eighth centuries in injecting fresh vigor into the languishing Christianity of the continent and carrying the light of the gospel to new lands. This is in large measure attributable to the fact that the Christian substratum, no matter how much overlaid, was securely in possession and continued to be an active force, though this was rarely talked about. The Sunday Mass remained the obvious keystone of the edifice of prayer and penance; its proper performance was taken very seriously. The presbyter who stumbled at the sacred words had to perform a penance, even to accept physical punishment. That section of the Mass containing the words of consecration was not without reason called the *periculosa oratio* (the dangerous prayer). On the chief feasts at any rate all were present, monks and clerics, including not a few priests, for the communal celebration. Among the communicants the layfolk would have been in a minority. The mystery of redemption was strongly affirmed and worthily treated, at least as an objective fact. It was given eloquent expression in a number of prayers. In the Antiphony of Banger indeed the Sunday still retained its Easter character, and the Irish Highcross dating from the eighth century with its arms entwined with the garland of victory shows that the center of gravity of Christian thought is as strongly affirmed as it was centuries previously when, as report goes, St. Patrick on his journeys through the land used to dismount from his chariot whenever he passed a cross.

Meeting of Two Traditions

With the eighth century the kingdom of the

Carolingians became the chief theatre of intellectual as well as spiritual life. Here (and to an extent also among their Anglosaxon precursors) two streams of tradition meet and mingle to become the matrix of the civilization of the Middle Ages. By the first of these was transmitted the intellectual output from the age of the great Church Fathers of the West as contained especially in the writings of Augustine and Jerome, but also Caesarius and Gregory the Great. It had come partly from the lands of the South by a direct route to Frankish territory and under Charlemagne had been substantially reinforced by the Italian scholars whom he had invited to his kingdom. The Lombardian Paul the Deacon, who had been entrusted with the task of determining the homilies of the Fathers which were to be used in the Office from then on, may be cited as a typical representative. The adoption of the Roman liturgy, final and decisive all along the line, lent support to this trend. From another quarter by way of the Anglosaxons came a similar influence. They had received the faith from Rome and developed it mightily, as seen in the career of Bede, doctor of the Church; and in their missions on the continent had spread it and given it new life.

The second stream, much less visible but all the more significant, is traceable to the world of thought of the Irish-Scottish monks and had already been absorbed by the Anglosaxon mission. Though fully conscious of his office as envoy of the Roman Church, and though he highly prized the Roman connection in which he had grown up, Winifrid (Boniface) in his intellectual and religious attitudes bore the stamp of Irish monastic thought rather than that of the Roman-Patristic type. This is not surprising: He had spent his life on the furthermost fringe of an Anglosaxon settlement which could boast of a Celtic stock whose Christianity reaching further back and with a religious outlook of its own was able to assert itself here precisely and powerfully.

It was much the same with Alcuin. His hometown, York, lay in that part of Northumbria where Celtic missionaries (from Hy-Jona) had worked successfully in the latter years of the seventh century and had founded new Christian settlements. Essential elements of the religious life were domiciled in this Irish-Scottish world and from there found entry to the mainland and to the general life of the Western Church. This can be gathered *inter alia* from the history of the inclusion of the *Credo* in the Mass. It turns up first in the West as a conclusion to the service of the Word, in the Irish Stowe Missal, in the version with which we are familiar today. Then it is attested to in England by Alcuin who speaks of it as already an obvious part of the liturgy with which he was evidently familiar from his early days. He succeeded in inducing Charlemagne to adopt it in his imperial chapel at Aachen; from there it found its way to Rome and to the world at large.

It is known that it was the Irish monks who first broke through the ruling that the sacrament of penance was to be received only once in life; a fact demonstrable on the continent in the eighth century in the practice of going to confession once each year. In later centuries this contributed to a changed attitude as regards a sense of sin, one less fretful.

Religious Life of the Period

If we try to form a picture of religious practice in this period we find that its outer contours as sketched in church institutions represent simply a continuance of what had gone on previously. On Sundays (to which a growing number of holydays of obligation were added) the faithful assembled in church. On solemn feast days the lords of the manor were also in attendance, though most of them had their own chaplain for the Sundays' Divine service was conducted in accordance with the Roman liturgical books with few mostly unconscious adaptations to local conditions. At episcopal sees and in other localities of some size there were clerical groups whose "canons" observed a fixed programme of life and of prayer in the traditional manner. A chief feature of the time were the well-organized monasteries which dotted the land. The Benedictine Rule with its balanced arrangement of the *Opus Dei* set the standard for them, first gradually and after the Reform Council of Aachen of 817, definitively.

Patterns of community service were thus stabilized by a tradition which had stood the test over the years. When, however, we investigate the prayer life of this period where religious sentiment finds a new expression of its own, another spirit is revealed. A double approach is open to us if we wish to get acquainted with the special religious features of the epoch and the way it prayed; first through the self-testimony of its leading personalities, as revealed in their literary work, and second by taking note of the surprising wealth of prayers that were committed to writing.

St. Boniface

Boniface's correspondence reveals a man for

whom the world is a valley of tears. He ill supports his personal defects and those of his fellows. For all that, however, his entire activity has prayer as its basis; a request for prayer recurs in almost every letter he writes: prayer for himself and for his work. He lays great store on the Confraternities of Prayer recently set in motion, through which help for the dead and success for his own activities will be assured. In this however, a consciousness of the fellowship of the faithful in Christ and in his Church fails to emerge. In general it can be said of Boniface that "his attitude is not determined by a joyous consciousness of our divine Sonship." "Grace for him is rather God's goodwill and favor which must be prayed for." Unlike St. Paul who sets forth life in Christ in positive, indicative terms, Boniface employs the moral imperative in his enforcement of ethical behavior. With him ritual ceremony plays no part; he is only remotely interested in theological considerations; "the stress falls on virtuous and meritorious action." And yet Boniface managed to lay the groundwork of a mighty enterprise in the service of the Church, one that was based on Church tradition and opened the way to that development which it was destined to attain in future years.

It is surprising how closely parallel is the picture we have of the spiritual outlook of Alcuin (d.804) who was fifty years Boniface's junior. Though he is interested in theological questions there is the same attitude to tradition which for him is "rather a faith acquired by learning and handed on to him" than personal possession. In his summary of Christian doctrine the emphasis lies less on salvation history than on the teaching with regard to the Blessed Trinity which gives the title to his work *De Fide Sanctae et Individuae*

Trinitatis. In his letters Christ is mentioned countless times, but the regular formula employed is *Christ Who is our Lord and God*; His divine dignity and his office as judge are placed in the foreground. The Pauline term *In Christ* becomes the element that unites him to mankind, but this is "no longer that human nature in which he resembles us, as brother of ours, but that divine clemency and gentleness which he turns toward us, to be almost cancelled by his justice." The predominant element in Alcuin's prayer life is the prayer of petition, petition for forgiveness of sin. When his friend Benedict of Aniane asked him one day what intention he prayed for when praying for himself he received the reply, "This is what I pray Christ for: That I may recognize my sins and do adequate penance for them."

In matters liturgical Alcuin was well versed. He played a decisive part in finally introducing the Roman Liturgy into France; and last but not least it is owing to his influence that serious efforts were undertaken during the Carolingian renaissance to get the people to take an active part once more in the liturgy. But equally clear is Alcuin's endeavor to introduce his own religious ideas into the supplementary additions he made to the liturgy. This is shown particularly in the prayer texts he composed for Votive Masses on weekdays. The idea of a Votive Mass where the special intentions (Vota) of the faithful were the occasion of the celebration was in principle quite justifiable; but its one-sided practice was bound rather to distract the attention from the essential meaning of the Eucharist. This tendency is observable in the epoch with which we are dealing; for example, when Isidore of Seville renders *eucharistia* by *bona gratia*, or when (contemporary with this) *missa* in the sense of blessing supplants the more ancient names for the Mass. In Alcuin's weekday Masses Friday still remains the day dedicated to the cross, but the theme for Sunday is no longer the resurrection but the Blessed Trinity. Saturday appears for the first time as Mary's day; the angels too have a formulary dedicated to them. A second series of formularies for each day of the week is completely attuned to penance; the prayers in them are petitions for divine aid in temptation and in the struggle with sin.

One is surprised at the sense of distinct remoteness from God, which permeates the thought and the prayers of these great men who rendered God's Church such signal service in their lifetime and played their part in the creation of a new epoch in its history. All this is in distinct contrast to what we have learned as the inheritance of previous epochs and was reproduced in the Roman Liturgy thanks to the conscientious way in which it was cherished and safeguarded, though evidently no longer put into practice. The leading feature of the liturgy is unequivocally that of Easter; its chief prayer is one of joyous gratitude for God's mercy and goodness. In every instance prayer is a confident approach to the Almighty as we look upward to Christ the mediator who lives and reigns in the glory of the Father. But here, on the other hand, an attitude prevails as though Christ, despite the number of times his name is invoked, had not yet come among us!

But the very way Christ is named and addressed betrays the point of rupture. St. Boniface's correspondence contains three prayers evidently meant to be inserted into the Mass as *apologias*. The first begins "Lord Jesus Christ, be propitious to me a sinner. For you alone are immortal and sinless. Lord, our God, you are blessed. . . . (Domine Jesu Christe, propitius esto mihi peccatori, quia tu es immortalis et sine peccato solus, Domine Deus noster, tu es benedictus. . .)". This closes mechanically with *per Dominum.* In the third of these prayers the opening *Domine* is repeated in the body of the prayer in the form: "Domine Jesu Christe, Filius Dei vivi Qui me creasti . . . (Lord Jesus Christ Son of the Living God who created me . . .)". We have here the same confusion between the predicates of God and of the Godman which constantly recurs in Alcuin's writings and goes to show that terms like *Christus Deus noster* had become a permanent formula.

Reaction to Arianism:

We are here confronted with the consequences of that over-emphasizing of the Godhead of Christ which was evoked by the struggle against Arianism and had begun to put its stamp upon the religious life of the West in the fifth and sixth centuries, beginning with Spain. The Arian Westgoths had set up as a formula of belief the words *Gloria Patri per Filium in Spiritu Sancto* (Glory to the Father through the Son in the Holy Spirit) thereby confessing the subordination of the Son to the Father and adhering to the tenets of Arianism. To meet this challenge the Catholic Church in Spain in its liturgical prayer was forced to stress in every possible way the equality in essence of the Son with the Father. Hence in the ancient Spanish liturgy, which was being developed precisely at this period, prayer was directed to the Son equally with the Father; even in the same prayer the form of address changes. The three Divine Persons are also addressed as such, or simply as the Blessed Trinity. Where allusion is made to the Godman who in the glory of the Father is head of the Church and our mediator, the *per Christum* remains, but it has become an empty formula, the meaning of which is scarcely attended to any longer. It is as though the distance between God and man had become a sundering chasm which could no longer be bridged by a mediator but only by reference to God's mercy (*per ineffabilem bonitatem Tuam etc.*). This is the type of piety which emerged as a result of the struggle with heresy in the Westgothic kindgom and continued to be regarded as the Catholic position in the flourishing church there even subsequent to the orthodox confession of the year 589.

A very brisk intercourse must have been maintained between Spain and Ireland to explain how these religious ideas were transmitted to the latter country. We have little evidence on the point but not a few indications. It is precisely this theological trend which confronts us there; only thus can we explain the puzzle that in Irish piety a pronounced Anti-arian christology and Anti-arian doctrine of the Trinity are in evidence, although Ireland had no truck at any time with Arians. When faith was no longer actively conscious of the redemption, and of the mediation effected by Christ, when the vast distance separating man from God oppressed his spirit with little now to mitigate the burden, the consciousness of his misery and sinfulness must have been overwhelming. It is no accident, apparently, that at the Synod of Tours (813) a new bodily posture at worship was expressly demanded for the first time, that of kneeling, "so that in this way we may crave God's mercy and the forgiveness of sins." A further consequence of all this was that people looked around for new sources of help, and that secondary mediators were now brought to the fore more assertively: Mary, the angels, the saints and relics.

Praying the Psalms

We observe this in the Carolingian prayer literature which had assumed surprising proportions. In Alcuin's closing years and in the following centuries a large number of *Libelli precum*, prayer books, had seen the light. We note particularly two collections of prayers and instructions on prayer which have come down to us among Alcuin's writings. One of these is made up of the *Officia per Ferias* composed in France in the first half of the ninth century; the other is entitled *De Psalmorum Usu* put together about the year 850 in Italy for monastic circles. Alcuin himself is the author of a shorter instruction on Praying the Psalms and of a writing addressed to Charlemagne, agreeing to fulfill his request to show how a *homo laicus* (a layman) living an active life should pray to the Lord during the usual prayer hours. In addition he is very probably responsible for a *Confessio peccatorum* which had a wide circulation and had also been composed for Charlemagne. It constitutes an almost frightening expression of consciousness of sin. Unsparingly, in the Irish mode, the user enumerates literally every organ of the body, from head to foot, confessing his guilt for all imaginable sins committed in thought, word and deed through the five senses, or for offenses against the eight deadly sins. It belongs to that literary genre of the *apologias* we have met in Irish monasticism and which in the meantime had become the prevailing type of formalized prayer. Alcuin's formula recurs once again as *confessio pura* in various localities; and not only that, but of new versions of it there is no lack. It was evidently assumed that such confessions of guilt, even for offenses that were never committed, served as a means of blotting out sin!

As against this, Alcuin's reply to Charlemagne's request brings us back to the world of attested tradition in the matter of prayer. Given that the demands he makes extend over the entire day they are certainly not modest; but usually there is question of brief prayer only. Linking up with the "seven times daily" recommendation, Alcuin demands such prayer at the first, second, third, sixth and ninth hours, at Vespers and at the twelfth hour; in addition a short prayer on rising which reads: "Lord Jesus Christ, Son of God, in your name I raise up my hands." Each time an Our Father should be added. In the first two prayer times and in the last two the content of the prayer is determined by the beginning and the close of the day's work. The three intermediate hours, corresponding to Terce, Sext and None are governed by early Christian tradition: They commemorate the three stages in the passion. At Terce the prayer runs: "Lord Jesus Christ, you were led at the third hour to the torment of the cross for the world's salvation, we humbly beseech you to grant us pardon for the evil we have committed and that we be preserved ever more from future evil." Alcuin mentions three other times for night prayer, but as he offers no texts for them, he apparently considers that this latter demand should not be taken seriously.

The relation of these hours of prayer to Christ's passion was not overlooked in later times too. This has long been attested to by the miniatures found in subsequent Books of Hours. Isolated prayer books too and instructions on prayer make mention of the connection, even in less remote times. But apparently the practice never attained genuine popularity despite the fact that in the spiritual literature of the following centuries all Horae are fairly often brought into relation with the events of Christ's life and passion. Important evidence from the ninth century goes to show that the layfolk also were not only expected to say their prayers morning and night (these included the customary Our Father and the Creed) but in addition to pray at the third, sixth and ninth hours. Bishop Jonas of Orleans around the year 830 reminded his people of this prescription and instructed King Pippin in the same sense.

Prayer-Life of the Period

Surveying how things stood in the matter of prayer during the Carolingian era, as far as we can determine it from literary sources, we can certainly say it included in general all the important components of Christian prayer: adoration, thanksgiving, intercession and petition for help in the struggle to observe the moral code. But the predominant note sounded here in heavy tones is almost invariably that of lament for sin committed. Liturgical texts, too, based on Roman and Gallican traditions are not wanting. Actually the *per Christum* phrase turns up occasionally even in new formulations. Two things strike us particularly, the strong emergence of the Trinitarian mystery and the predominant role assigned to the Psalter. Profession of faith in the Blessed Trinity is given striking emphasis.

It is as though the world were still full of Arians, or at least as if people were still living in the days of the Toletan Synods. A significant phenomenon is prayer addressed to the Trinity hitherto foreign to the Roman liturgy. It suffices to draw attention to two prayers in the liturgy of our Mass (as observed till recently), derived from the Sacramentary of Amiens (ninth century): *Suscipe, sancta Trinitas; Placeat tibi, sancta Trinitas* (Receive, Holy Trinity; May it please you, Holy Trinity). Often at the beginning of a fairly long prayer we have a complicated, anxiously worded Trinitarian confession. Evidently the *fides Trinitatis* had to be expressed in accurate terms if the prayer were to be acceptable. This anxiety is voiced in a formula, otherwise christological in content, which is attached to the confession of sin: Following on the crucial sentences the following words occur: "This is the faith by which I express my belief in you. If I am believing properly, all is well; but in case something is lacking I pray you not to regard the words I have spoken but what I wished to say." Such are the opening words of a prayer for help in combatting temptation. The prayer is underpinned by a sort of litany invoking saints of the Old and New Testaments, followed by the appeal: "Dominator, Domine Deus, qui es Trinitas, unus Pater in Filio et Filius in Pater cum Spiritu Sancto" (Sovereign, Lord God, you are three-in-one, Father in the Son and Son in the Father along with the Holy Spirit). In other cases the Divine Persons are individually invoked: "Rogo te, Pater; deprecor te, Fili; obsecro te, Spiritus Sancte" (I ask you, Father, I beg you, Son; I implore you, Holy Spirit).

This could occur even in three successive prayers that had no connection with each other and were addressed in turn: (Oratio) ad Patrem, ad Personam Filii, ad Personam Spiritus Sancti. This might appear consistent were it not followed by: "Oratio ad Sanctam Trinitatem, Oratio ad Dominum Jesum Christum" and then by "obsecratio ad sanctam Dei Genetricem, ad sanctos apostolos, ad venerabilem Benedictum, ad plures confessores." As a consequence it became usual in this area after the opening address to Christ in the ancient litany (as also in the later litanies derived from it) to add the three Divine Persons. A further consequence drawn in the tenth century affected church Art; it no longer depicted Christ according to his human nature under a human appearance exclusively, but in association with the Father and finally with the Holy Spirit also—a manner of representat on which was only partially superseded in the twelfth century through the notion of the *Throne of Mercy*. (Gnadenstuhl)

Trinitarian Current

If here the world of faith threatened to be broken up into "Persons" who have each in turn to be worshiped, the opposite trend, namely the homage to be paid the unity of the Divine Persons (their unity of essence or at least their equality of essence) was stressed by changing the mode of address in the course of the same prayer. This peculiarity we noted above with reference to the Spanish liturgy. A prayer starts, for example: "Sancte Pater" and then becomes "Clemens Trinitas" (Merciful Trinity); or it begins addressing Christ and straightaway he is described as "Creator," Domine Jesu Christe, qui me dignatus fuisti creare ad imaginem tuam" (Creator Lord Jesus Christ who deigned to create me in your image). In this way very questionable combinations arose like "Auxiliatrix es tu mihi, sancta Trinitas; tu es sacerdos in aeternum." "Holy Trinity, you are my helper, you are a priest for ever." How strong this Trinitarian current became is seen in the fact that it succeeded in making several changes in the Roman liturgy which had been adopted in the land of the Franks. We have already drawn attention to the two prayers to the Blessed Trinity found in our daily Mass Ordo. At the turn of the eighth century the symbol *Quicumque*, with its pronounced probing into the mystery of the Trinity, became an integral part of the Sunday Prime and then, for a long period, of the daily Prime.

The preface of the Trinity appears for the first time in the ninth century in the St. Gall manuscript of the later Gelasianum. It gradually asserted itself as a Sunday preface in Rome but only in 1759—a delayed action! As is known, not only the feast of the Blessed Trinity but its traditional Office was also composed in the lands of the North. In keeping with the Gallico-Spanish custom of providing liturgical Oratios even where Christ is addressed, the *per Dominum* of the closing formula is changed to *Qui vivis et regnas cum Deo Patre* in not a few Roman Oratios which offer an opening for such (redemptio tua, adventus tuus, apostolus tuus etc.). Thus the mediatorial office of the glorified Godman meets with little comprehension.

As appears from the foregoing, a serious loss of definite orientation touching a matter of importance must be registered. Nevertheless, in the last resort tradition remains the determining factor in Christian prayer. Through the contours of the risen Christ living on in his glorified state as Godman are almost absorbed and dissolved by the supreme majesty of his Godhead; yet the cross shines out still in its old-world splendor as it did in Alcuin's world of piety. It remains forever the sign of victory, the throne of the King, the jewel of the world. This central place is claimed for it not alone in Carolingian art; in the Celtic Highcross of Ireland especially it retains a far wider validity; it is vindicated too in many a prayer and greeting addressed to the holy cross, and not the least in the religious outlook associated with the Psalms in that period, to which we must now turn our attention.

Division of the Psalms

In the older form of monasticism, particularly the Irish, the Psalms were appraised chiefly from their character as sacred word: They were prayed through in their sequence *currente psalterio* and in as great a number as possible without much attention being paid to the content of the individual sacred song. However, in the two sizeable Introductions to Praying the Psalms in the Carolingian epoch an earnest effort is made to bring their content to the fore, incidentally making a meaningful selection of them possible (as far as free choice allowed outside the prescribed Office). One of these introductions *De Psalmorum Usu* begins with a foreword for which Alcuin himself is responsible. With evident enthusiasm he extols the virtue of the psalms to which: "It is impossible to do justice provided they are recited not with the lips only but with interior relish to the praise of Almighty God." Alcuin distinguishes nine possible chief heads or themes into which they can be divided: They open up a wide prospect of Christian piety to our gaze though a fairly somber note peculiar to Alcuin's mentality is not lacking. It will be rewarding to indicate some essential features of his choice.

1. Penance: this purpose is served by the Seven Penitential Psalms, known as such from the days of Cassiodorus.
2. Spiritual joy: Psalms 16,24,53,66,69,70,85.
3. Praise and thanksgiving for God's benefits in the Old and New Testament: either the Alleluia Psalms or Psalms 71-73,109-119 etc.
4. In temptation and desolation: Psalms 21,63,67.
5. In times of boredom with life or of longing for Heaven: Psalms 41,62,83.
6. In distress: Psalms 12,43,50,54,70.
7. In good days: Psalms 33,102,103,144, *Canticum Benedicite*
8. On God's law: Psalm 118.
9. On God's working for our salvation, beginning with the Prophets up to the Lord's passion, resurrection and ascension: with no reference, meaning the entire Psalter.

The collection of the psalms at the head of which Alcuin's instructions are transmitted to us is less in keeping with them than the somewhat older collection of the *Officia per ferias*. The selected psalms are here distributed among the days of the week, beginning with Sunday. The number of psalms apportioned to each day varies from three to seventeen: the Penitential Psalms are allocated to Mondays. Some further themes of Alcuin recur with the like allocation: Praise and thanksgiving for God's benefits along with the Alleluia Psalms on Sundays, those said in times of distress on Wednesdays, on good days, on Thursdays, in times of boredom with life and longing for heaven on Saturdays. There is a second series of psalms for Saturday: The choice here is evidently determined by the association of that day with Mary, just as in Alcuin's weekday Masses psalm 44 is allotted to honoring her, psalm 18 is assigned to the apostles, psalm 32 to the martyrs, psalm 123 to the confessors. For Fridays an attempt is made to bring the psalms into line with Alcuin's final theme, namely salvation history. A psalm each is devoted to Christ's passion (ps 34), to his resurrection (ps 3) and his ascension (ps 8). Then the entire Psalter is added in the shape of Beda's *Collectio Psalterii*.

In another respect also the *Officia per Ferias* gives evidence of a developed form of psalmody. Each psalm is followed by a few versicles and an Oratio of Roman or Gallican character, in the content of which in most cases a Christian echo can be detected. So there too in the first half of the ninth century the ancient psalter collects survive.

The *De Psalmorum Usu* departs a little further from Alcuin's instructions: the themes offered in sixteen sections cover his only in part. In addition there are intercessions for the living and the dead. In each section, after the designation of the psalm, follow the Lord's Prayer and a fairly long prayer or several prayers of the type described above, for which an island model also exists. The whole is furnished with a prayer supplement.

The Carolingian zest for meaningful psalmody

is also given expression in two adaptations of the psalms which Alcuin forwarded to his friend, Archbishop Arno of Salzburg, in 802. In an accompanying letter he mentions a *Psalterium Parvum* designated as Bede's psaltery which "praises God in sweet verses"; also a *Hymnus vetus de quindecim psalmis graduum*. In the first of these works, for which older models had already been in existence, one or other significant verse is selected from each of the one hundred and fifty psalms to make an abridged psalter. The second work is also preserved; it consists of fifteen quatrains based on the fifteen Gradual Psalms but of little artistic merit.

5
The World of Aniane and Cluny

The centuries following on the Carolingian epoch were characterized by an effort to maintain the intellectual gains already acquired and to develop and extend them further. The undoubted leaders in this movement were the monasteries. The constitution and life style proper to them were adopted in many points by the clergy, particularly after the Council of Reform of the year 817. Where feasible, clerics were expected to lead a life in community as canons. This meant a shared prayer, consisting of the full seven Horae of the Office. The pioneer in this development, Chorodegang of Metz (d. 766), seems to have taken the Roman basilica-monastery as his model.

The prime mover in the work of reorganizing monastic life at the Council was Benedict of Aniane (d.821)—in Lower Languedoc, France–the friend of emperor Ludwig the Pious. At the latter's instance the Rule of St. Benedict became the sole monastic rule throughout the Carolingian empire. However, it seemed impractical to the reformer to limit the prayer arrangement strictly to what the ancient Regula prescribed, with the result that some additions were introduced in the practice of prayer in his model monastery of Karneli-minster near Aachen, to which other monasteries had to conform.

Before Matins began, the monks of his monastery came to the chapel and visited the several altars, following a custom of earlier times: at each altar a Pater Noster and Creed (the morning prayer of baptized Christians) were said; then they took their places in the choir and recited in silence five psalms for the living, with a closing Oratio, then five for the dead, and finally five for the recently deceased. These were evidently the fifteen Gradual Psalms. Visits to the altars were repeated before Prime and after Compline. After Compline each monk had to recite ten psalms in winter and five in summer. The custom of making these visits in the morning and before retiring at night which were usually associated with a *trina oratio*, a triple prayer varying in wording for the different intentions was maintained in many cases as a voluntary practice in the monasteries during the subsequent centuries; its derivatives survive to the present. So do the thrice-five Gradual Psalms, each with its closing prayer. They form an addition to the Office and, as a rule are recited in common. During Lent they are a matter of obligation for choir prayer even where the clergy are concerned.

Additions to the Office

How did it come about that these not inconsiderable additions were made to St. Benedict's Office, additions which were to be further increased? Evidently a new element had asserted itself, that of intercessory prayer for the monastery's benefactors living and dead. Intercession had always been associated with prayer, intercession for the multiple intentions of Christendom and for its various groups and classes. In the form of prayer dialogue within and without the Mass intercessions preceded a concluding Oratio said by the priest. A novelty was that the intercessory prayers said here were meant for a definite circle of people and that a special block of the psalms was assigned for the purpose. The explanation is to be found in the history of most Merovingian and Carolingian monasteries. As a rule they were no longer the result of a community coming together to live as monks and had erected the monastic buildings with their own hands; they were rather the product of charitable endowments of wealthy landowners, including even kings like the Burgundian Sigismund whom we have already met, founder of Agaunum-St. Morice (in Valais, Switzerland). The return on the part of the monastery took the form of a vastly augmented and unbroken recitation of the psalms by groups of monks who relieved each other in turn at a work redounding, it is true, to God's honor but at the same time having in mind the spiritual welfare of founders and benefactors. A problem arose when the ceaseless recitation of the Psalter day and night (or day only, as at St. Riquier) could so easily sink to the level of a purely external performance. This was likely enough when the 150 psalms *currente psalterio* were repeated from beginning to end, over and over again. Benedict of Aniane saw the need of finding a solution in the additions referred to, additions which before long were further enlarged. *Psalmi speciales* (a flexible term) were enjoined. A daily Office for the Dead, consisting of Vespers, a Nocturn and Matins was introduced, possibly by the reformer himself or at any rate not much after his time. In the tenth century it was celebrated in all monasteries. In addition *Psalmi familiares* came into being, each made up of one, two or more psalms which were linked to the different Horae as intercessory prayers for the friends of the monastery. During the long winter nights in many monasteries the traditional fifteen morning Gradual Psalms were extended to twice their length by the addition of psalms 134-150. As a further addition in the morning or after Prime the seven Penitential Psalms with litany were recited. At Cluny during the Lenten season two *Psalmi prostrati* were added after each Hora, and all this in addition to the lengthy series of versicles which were linked up with the psalms. Finally, individual devotional themes were selected and a special psalmody was devoted to them. In the South-German monastery to which we owe the Einsiedeln manuscript the Matins of All Saints (*Matutina de omnibus sanctis*) was added to the Office for the Dead. And then in the mid-tenth century a Hora in honor of the mother of God was introduced which in the following century became the Little Office *de Beata Virgine*.

Cluny, Center of Monastic Piety

In the eleventh century Cluny—in the Rhone Valley—was a convergent center for all those forms of devotion which, incidentally, filled out the monastic order of time. The biographer of abbot Odo (d.942) eulogizes the zeal for prayer which flourished in those days when more than 138 psalms were recited daily. Indeed, if all the statements on the point are to be taken literally, each monk was obliged to get through 215 psalms daily (this figure is for a somewhat later date). In any event this constituted a single day's performance which Benedict would have scarcely assigned to his monks during an entire week. Thus the *laus perennis* which Benedict of Aniane had intended to repeal had returned under another form. The founder's intention to have something of lasting value performed for their souls' welfare, and the agelong monastic ideal of living completely for God, met once more in a conception, it is true, of the efficacy of prayer, but one which St. Augustine would not have countenanced. And yet under the hard crust of such choir routine, genuine prayer must have been carried on in Cluny, and God must have been sought and found in earnest, in a monastery too where not only corporal work was eschewed but almost every other extra activity of a mental nature as well. Otherwise, it is impossible to account for the spiritual renewal which emanated from that monastery, a renewal which encompassed the Church at large and is part of her history.

On the other hand, during the period we are considering, the feeling must have been reinforced that the quantitive effort which the recital or the chanting of the sacred words of the biblical Psalter entailed did not yet represent the ideal of correct prayer. Hence measures of various kinds were taken to meet the difficulty. The supplementary Offices, the product of a selection of psalms which would be meaningful were designed to override the mere working through long series of psalms *currente psalterio*. The sequences of versicles which in many cases had been introduced into the Office and preceded an Oratio consisted of specially chosen verses. Similarly a Little Psaltery such as the *Psalterium Bedae* referred to above aimed at selecting those verses which would appeal more to the user. The headings made out for the psalms with a

New Testament title, as well as the addition of a psalm collect after each psalm or a series of psalms was, as we have seen, a long-traditional practice. That the *officia per ferias* of the ninth century are not the final attestation for this is shown by the Commentary on the Psalms of bishop Bruno of Wurzburg (d.1045) who reproduces in essentials Cassiodorus' Commentary on the Psalms. However, in doing so he shortens Cassiodorus' somewhat and on occasion supplements it by citing other Fathers and introducing a traditional New Testament title for each psalm, with an Oratio added.

Hymnody

A new element, evidently meant to serve the same purpose of making prayer more interior and more compatible with Christian overtones, came increasingly to the fore in the ninth century. This was a new upsurge of hymnody and its utilization for the Office. An early precedent for it had emerged in the East where it was more widely diffused than in the West. In the responsorial psalmody of the Syrians the refrain verse was further developed to form a stanza, and the repetition of the refrain was replaced by extra stanzas. Thus arose the Syrian *enjane*. The same phenomenon occurred in the Greek Church in the biblical *Cantica* (Odes) which from early times formed part of the concluding section of Matins. From them the Greek *Canones* arose, compositions of a high poetic and religious quality. Finally, this new element became such a favorite with both Syrians and Greeks that in the Office current in the Byzantine are only the first verse of the original psalm or canticle was left, and eventually even this was in many cases no longer sung.

With the result that in the East the weight of the poetical material actually stifled the psalmody in the day-hours of the Office.

Developments in the West were not carried that far, though the hymn found an early place in St. Benedict's Office. It appears now in the general Office either at the head of the Horae or (in Matins and Vespers) replaces a former responsory, in this approximating somewhat to the oriental trend. What significance hymnody had atained in the following centuries of the Middle Ages as enrichment and interpretation of feast days in Office and Mass (Sequences) and in the mounting cult of Mary can be gauged from the medieval collection of Latin hymns which in a German repertory runs into fifty-five volumes.

Lay Participation

To what extent was the general body of the faithful affected by this intense prayer life in the monasteries which, reaching beyond the collegiate chapter, was largely shared by the secular clergy? The language barrier from the very beginning constituted a difficulty in the evangelization of the Germanic tribes. It now began to affect the Romance domain as well. It was bound, so one would have thought, to exclude the people from a sharing in the ancient cathedral-Horae especially in the elaborate, clericalized form they had assumed. That is not absolutely the case. The faithful came to church on Sundays and attended the Latin Mass where the deeper import of the rite of which they were conscious, the ceremonial full of animation and the allegorical interpretation of the whole rite in the light of Christ's life and passion, compensated to a certain extent for a faulty understanding of the words, an understanding to which they scarcely aspired. But they came also to Matins and Vespers. The change of the word Matutinum to the German *Mettine* which is traceable to the twelfth century is indicative of a broader interest on the people's part. As witness to a custom still prevailing in that century we can cite a passage in the *Nibelungenlied* where it is reported that Kriemhilde, one morning in front of her door, found Siegfried's dead body as she was on her way to *Mettine*, a ceremony "which Lady Kriemhilt very seldom missed" (der diu vrouwe Kriemhilt vil selten deheine verlac)—17 Aventiure, Strophe 1004.

Alcuin and Charles the Bald

The traditional ideal of prayer survived in theory, if not always in practice, and here we must distinguish between those who enjoyed a certain higher level of Christian formation and the mass of the simple people. In respect to the former we are fortunate in possessing in the prayer book of Charles the Bald (d.877), two generations precisely after Charlemagne, a new draft of that prayer arrangement which Alcuin drew up for his master. Beginning with an introduction, it contains Alcuin's full day's programme for the seven Horae and their accompanying prayer texts; only the Our Father which is linked with each is not mentioned. On the other hand, the author of the new work takes cognizance also of the prayers to be said three times during the night which are mentioned in the introduction. For this purpose he assigns to Compline three psalms, an Our Father and Creed and two additional short prayers. Included (definitely for voluntary use only) is a complete plan for praying the psalms in which we meet again Alcuin's instruction on choosing those that suit the soul's varied conditions and moods of which we have spoken. Then we have a comprehensive Litany and a number of scattered prayers of the type usual in those days including Alcuin's more extended *Confiteor*. Concern for the liturgy also is voiced in quite a significant manner. The princely worshiper is supplied with prayers *quando offertis ad Missam* (when you offer the oblata at Mass), with the response also to the *Orate Fratres* and a short *Confiteor* before handing over the personal oblata and before receiving Holy Communion, and in addition two Communion prayers; all in all Alcuin's school at its best, with a stress laid on extended psalmodic elements. At this period the Psalter was generally a stable component of a fully-furnished *Liber precum* (prayer book) for the educated layman.

Psalmody and Lay Piety

How far did the simple faithful share now in this prayer cult? Were some individual psalms made available, perhaps to them, selections from the Psalter which occupied such a prominent place in the prayer life of monks and clerics? To judge from old German translations of the psalms which have survived, the answer must be in the negative. They bear no relation as regards bulk to the Old High German *Beichten* (variations of the Confiteor), and besides they do not concern those psalms which, from our experience of earlier centuries, might presumably have had a certain popularity. Rather we are back once more to the domain of monastery-school and clerical training-ground. At most we find in the old Alemann psalms, dated 820, elements of a practice of prayer that is at once most fully alive and most deeply rooted in antiquity. They consist in the main of a selection from the Gradual Psalms. Sections from psalms 107,108,113 and 114 are followed, after a lacuna in transmission, by psalms 123,124,128,129 and 130. About the year 1000 Notker, the German made a complete translation, with commentary, of the Psalter. We have in addition some fairly short fragments dating not too far back. More often early English fragments of the Psalter are to be met with; but the full translation of the Psalter dates to the ninth century. At most, verses from individual psalms may have been in current use. In a list of *Redemptions* which appears as a supplement to the work of Regino von Pruem (d.915) entitled *De Synodalibus Causis* a number of psalms, genuflections and Our Fathers is fixed as substitute for a fast day. If, however, the person does not know the psalms he prostrates himself one hundred times, saying in the meantime the *Miserere mei Deus* and *Dimitte, Domine, peccata mea* (Have mercy on me, God; forgive me my sins, Lord). But even this latter requirement is not maintained: in the Penance Book of Burchard of Worms (d.1025) one hundred Our Fathers are substituted for those ejaculations. In much the same way the *Consuetudines* of the Farfa abbey—25 miles north of Rome—(eleventh century) prescribe the recital of fifty psalms for a monk's deceased relatives; but if he is not familiar with the psalms he can substitute a *Miserere mei, Deus,* and if that is beyond him, let him say Pater Nosters.

Early German Texts

Nourishment for the people's prayer life was mainly supplied by the basic Christian formulae, the Pater Noster and Creed, German versions of which are among the most ancient documents of Old High German. In many cases the confession of faith is, to a surprising degree, closely associated with a confession of sin (confiteor). The name given by German scholars to these Old High German texts is *Glaube und Beicht* (Faith and Confession). This is partly traceable to the practice in vogue since the eighth century of going once a year to confession; the priest let the penitent say first the Our Father and the Confession of Faith; then the usual formula for the confession of sin could follow—a practice which was maintained in subsequent centuries. We also have Carolingian prayer texts in which a confession of faith precedes a confession of sin.

Further texts in Old High German, in the so-called *Weissenburger Katechismus* contain the Athanasian Creed (which in subsequent centuries recurs surprisingly often) as well as the Gloria in excelsis. Apart from the basic texts mentioned, the prayer life of the people would have been confined to a more or less reverential sharing in the divine service. An active sharing which was the aim in the Carolingian renaissance cannot have been retained for long. Responses even to the priest's prayers, and the acclamations, must soon have been silenced. Still the faithful were accustomed to answer the Kyrie eleison in the litanies; and this gave birth to the *Leise* and therewith the beginnings of the German hymn; the earliest example being the Petrus Hymn.

Libelli Precum

A feature of the religious thought of the ninth century to the eleventh century were the *Libelli Precum,* collections of prayers and instructions on the art of prayer which we met when treating of the Carolingian epoch. As evidence of their continued vogue it suffices to point to the prayer book published as a Manual for St. John Gualbert (d.1073), founder of Vallombrosa Abbey (near Florence). André Wilmart made use of this publication as starting point for a wide-ranging research. He was able to show that the traditional attribution of the book to the distinguished abbot could well mean that he used and treasured it but that in the layout of its contents and in several individual texts it corresponded accurately with ninth-century conditions: Numerous passages in it cover the same ground as the collection *De Psalmorum Usu* which appeared in upper Italy about the year 850 and it is even more closely related to a similar collection of prayers written between 860 and 880, which originated in Nonatola near Modena.

Another offshoot from the same parent stock and dating from the same time is the *Libellus Precum* from the monastery of Fleury on the Loire. In the texts which form a special feature in it we find the same accusation of sin, the same meticulous confession of the Blessed Trinity, the same predilection for specific prayers addressed to the Divine Persons. These occasionally assume the larger form of a litany (in the Fleury Libellus more than two hundred saints are invoked) and are interspersed with prayers which also find a place in the liturgy.

John of Fécamp

We have to mention here a name which represents a certain final term in the literature of the *Libelli Precum* and which at the same time extends its influence far beyond it: John of Fécamp, born about the year 990 who died in 1078 as abbot of Fécamp near Rouen. His intellectual output, attributed to Augustine and Alcuin among others, has been restored to him in our century. His best-known production is the prayer *Summe Sacerdos* named until recently "Oratio S. Ambrosii," divided among the seven days of the week and reproduced at the beginning of the Missale Romanum; it forms part of the Praeparatio ad Missam. It is still couched in the language of the *Apologias* (formulas of self-accusation) but the accusation which runs through it is mitigated by a genuine Christian confidence. His other writings in prayer form resemble so much the Carolingian type of prayer that Wilmart wished at first to attribute to him the authorship of *De Psalmorum Usu*.

But what is there expressed only in inchoate terms regarding God's infinite majesty and the adoring wonderment which it evokes in the worshiper is in John's *Confessio Fidei* developed and amplified in recurring variants by a brilliant mind, by one too who was a man of intense prayer. In amazing contrasts the essential transcendence of God, the surpassing grandeur of the Divine Nature Three-in-One is glorified in a language which unconsciously recalls to intervening centuries the *Confessions* and *Soliloquies* of an Augustine. A somewhat fretful anxiety in expressing properly the Trinitarian confession, and the repetitious address to the Trinity in constantly evolving language, run through these prayers too; but there is no trace of a confounding of the notions of God and Christ, or any vagueness in the invocations of the prayers. The *Confessio Fidei* is a survey of the Christian world of faith expressed in the language of prayer. In the first section God One and Three is treated; in the second the mysteries of the Verbum Incarnatum; in the third the other articles of the Creed. Finally a fourth has to do with the mystery of the Blessed Eucharist which in 1044 was threatened by Berengar's dissentient attitude. The *Meditationes* reveal a similar pattern. A section is devoted to a dialogue with Christ; the saints too who have attained the goal of their earthly pilgrimage are invoked once. Then the prayer reverts to an admiring contemplation of the Divine Majesty.

It is no matter for surprise that the prayers of the abbot of Fécamp were assured of a popularity with future generations. Not that the theological balance and particularly the central position of the mystery of Christ, as evidenced in the documents on prayer which we have cited from this period, were not to be found elsewhere. In circles where the New Testament was read with a perceptive mind and the world of the Fathers explored, a more lucid perspective was bound to emerge. André Wilmart cites a *Symbolum*—prayer composed by a monk from the monastery of Metz about the year 1100 which combines religious warmth with a clarity of expression which does full justice to Christian thinking. Wilmart regards it as evidence of Christian tradition at its best and extols its fine qualities in enthusiastic terms. As a fact it is little more than the felicitous development of a more ancient text. For in the Collection *De Psalmorum Usu*, between the texts of the confession of guilt and the accusation we come across a *confessio* which surprises the reader straightaway by its theological and religious clarity. It begins with the invocation *Domine Deus* and professes belief in the Unity and Trinity of God and the sending of the Son in the Person of Christ. It then turns to Christ and confesses to the events of his childhood and his passion which are briefly described up to his ascension and his coming again. It concludes with the following profession: "I believe you have said: I will not the death of the sinner (Ez 33:11) and "In heaven there will be more joy over one sinner . . ." (Lk 15:7). The *confessio* is taken from the Commentary on the Benedictine Rule by Paul the Deacon (d. 799) who was rightly esteemed as an expert in the writings of the Fathers. There may have been many men of prayer of this type, since there were many who used the *lectio divina* to steep themselves in the literature of the great Church Fathers and from them drew nourishment and enrichment for their spiritual lives. And yet they failed to influence the religious atmosphere of the age.

6
From the Eleventh Century Onward

It is a long established fact that in the cultural history of the Middle Ages, around the turn of the eleventh and twelfth centuries, something new emerged, and this despite the permanence of external conditions of living. The same is true in the realm of the spiritual life as well. It is most marked where its central theme, the mystery of Christ, is concerned. Heretofore, the work of redemption was in the forefront, the cross as a victory over sin, the risen Lord inaugurating a new creation. Now, however, a sense of the concrete suddenly reveals itself; interest is focused on the person of him who achieved the redemption, on the external facts of his appearance in this world and his career as reported in the gospels. The thoughts of the worshiper still continue to revolve about the central themes which are emphasized in the Apostles Creed and are celebrated during the two chief feasts of the year, Christmas and Easter, namely the entry of God's Son into the world, his passion and resurrection. But now it is predominantly the empirical components of the mystery which engage men's loving contemplation: The birth from Mary the virgin and the passion in its several phases, which is no longer interpreted as the *beata passio* (the blessed passion) but the bitter passion before all else; Christ is the *Christus secundum carnem;* the spiritual perspective is no longer that of Easter but is focused on Christmas and Good Friday.

Reaction to Arianism

This goes to show that it is a misleading simplification on the part of French authors, beginning with Père Rousselot (d.1915) to insist on characterizing the process somewhat as follows: At long last the humanity of Christ had entered the purview of Christian piety, whereas hitherto attention had been almost exclusively centered on his divinity. The reverse is rather the case. This alone is true, that the favorite theme for contemplation was now the Lord's human nature during the period before his resurrection. His continued life after Easter, his glorious transfigured life as man, which was the object of the contemplation of the early Christians, was indeed still conceptually known but it was no longer a living factor in the consciousness of the faithful. And yet it was that glorified life which was to the fore with St. Paul and in all patristic thinking. This change of perspective was already long at work; in previous chapters we have seen its preliminary stages. It began as a reaction to the Arian denial of Christ's true divinity; and in the contemplation of a still-living Lord it led to the avoidance of any element by which he could appear to be less than the Father, namely his human nature and therewith his office as mediator. It led also to a widespread elimination of the *per Christum* on the one hand, and on the other to a ceaseless stressing of the equality in essence and the oneness in essence of the three Divine Persons. In this shift of perspective we can detect the first phase of the piety peculiar to the Middle Ages.

We enter on a second phase around the eleventh century. Here, from the same basic assumptions, conclusions of a different kind were drawn. In the Christian world of faith the figure of the glorified Godman is obscured and dimmed to a greater and greater degree. A double effect followed on this: One was that all the greater effort was made to look around for secondary mediators, the other was a total concentration on what indisputably remained of Christ's human nature, the earthly life which he had assumed. It cannot be denied that a certain primitive instinct of the sense-bound, medieval German mind, and especially its desire to have a visual perception of holiness, favored such a development. Yet in one point the mounting devotion to the passion is proof of a definite permanence of tradition, namely in the veneration of the Holy Cross which, uniting in itself elements, old and new, reached its climax in the eleventh century. In earlier times, as we have seen, chants of praise and salutation to the cross were not an occasional feature of Christian piety. Now, however, a regular literature on the theme comes into being. The *adoratio crucis* on Good Friday had taken shape already in the Romano-Germanic Pontificale of Mainz (950) to form an imposing rite which survives today, but only in its outlines. From the beginning it took for granted that the people had their share in the ceremony. For each of the three genuflections by which the cross is approached on Good Friday, a fairly long prayer was provided. In the eleventh century, appended to the Farfa Psalter, the supply of prayers for this and other occasions when adoring the cross (orationes ad crucem salutandam in Parasceve aliisque temporibus dicendae) go to make up an Office of good measure. About the same period in the Nonantula monastery the supply is further augmented and interwoven with stanzas from psalm 118: These consist in hymns of greeting to the *vexillum sanctae crucis,* prayers of unequal length in which Christ is addressed for the most part; also orationes and antiphons from the liturgy some traditional, others recently composed, treating in various tones the same theme, thanksgiving for the redemption and humble petition for pardon for sinful humanity. Despite the warmth of feeling with which they are instinct we still note a feature which also inspires the parallel Church art of the Ottonian epoch: not the high cross with its symbolism is portrayed but the Crucified One, the Crucifixus in regal attitude, the Sovereign who overthrows sin and death, the *Victor Rex*, as he is named in the Easter Sequence of Wipo (d. after 1048).

In the prayers of homage to the Holy Cross emotional participation already plays quite a large part; but a further step in the same direction is taken from the tenth century onward, the dramatization of the key moment in the story of the passion. In some localities, as a conclusion to the exacting liturgy traditional to Good Friday, a crucifix or even the sacramental Body of the Lord is laid in the tomb to the accompaniment of prayers and chants. A parallel custom is the dramatic announcement on Easter morning that CHRIST IS RISEN—a ceremony which marks the beginning of the Easter plays.

Devotion to the Passion

This eagerness for a visual approach to the passion finds a fresh outlet for prayerful participation in compassionate grief for the suffering redeemer. This type of prayer and meditation is given early expression in St. Anselm's writings when he was abbot of Bec (1063-1093). Anselm was not only an acute theologian but definitely a man of prayer. His body of writing includes a group of *Orationes sive Meditationes*—comprehensive prayers meant to be read and reflected upon, which pass over to meditation and from there back to prayer. As a fact, it is in this stylized prayer that the saint actually composed some of his theological works. He was anxious that his prayers or meditations, whose purpose was to foster a love and a fear of God and incite to self-examination, should be read not *cursim et velociter* (cursorily and hurriedly) but in a collected mood and so far only as was calculated to kindle in the reader an *affectus orandi* (a disposition for prayer). This affectus or devout attitude is all that he is interested in whether he is depicting the perils of a sinful life or is expressing his amazement at the self-immolation of the redeemer or extolling the dignity of the Virgin-Mother or the moral grandeur of sainthood. With particular fervor he treats of the sufferings of Christ as he addresses his own soul in these terms: "How is it possible that the sword of grief did not pierce you also? Were you not present there (on Calvary) too and suffered the lance to pierce the redeemer's heart. . . . How came it that you were not drunk with bitter tears as he drank the bitter gall?"

Anselm had set the tone for this kind of literature on prayer, which probably explains why such a mass of it was transmitted to subsequent centuries under his name. Henceforward, the passion of Christ is the favorite theme of Christian piety: leading to the large-scale pilgrimages to the Holy Sepulchre and eventually to the Crusades. Special forms of devotion were created to honor the sufferings of Christ; the most ancient of these was probably devotion to his five wounds. Peter Damian (d. 1072) was one of the first writers to make mention of it: "The Body of the Lord is pierced five times over that we may be healed from the sins which enter through our five senses."

Devotion to Mary Theotókos

The tendency to dwell on the details of the earthly life of Jesus becomes more and more perceptible in the new predilection for the Christmas mystery and the veneration of the Mother of God. Mary had always been specially honored in the Catholic Church, but her name and fame were definitely associated with the redemptive event: she was the *Theotókos;* her image stood invariably for a certain hieratic dignity and austerity. Now, however, she herself became more and more an independent theme for veneration, and the winning features of the Virgin Mother came to the fore. Though in earlier days one was also familiar with individual invocations to the Mother of God, it is only now that *The Little Office of Mary* appears primarily as a supplement to the choral Office proper. Bishop Ulric of Augsburg (d.973) and Peter Damian (d.1072) both attest to the fact. Of the former it is reported in his *Life* (c.3) that in addition to the daily Office in choir he recited each day, where possible, a series of prayers, one in honor of Mary, the Mother of God, a second in honor of the Holy Cross, and a third in honor of all the saints. Peter Damian mentions with approval an Office of Mary consisting of seven Horae. The members of the Premonstratentian Order, lately founded, were obliged to recite daily the new Office of Mary. Other associations followed suit. Peter Damian is also the first to testify that the Ave Maria (the angelical salutation to Mary, combined with that of her cousin Elizabeth; Lk 1:28,42) had become a favorite prayer with the people. From then on similar testimonies multiply and around 1210, beginning with the *Statuta Synodalia* of Paris, episcopal ordinances express the wish that the faithful, in addition to the reciting of the Our Father and the Creed, should also learn the Ave Maria.

The Akathist Hymn

The eleventh century marks the period when veneration of the Mother of God, rather latent hitherto, erupted in a multiplicity of forms. The fact has long since been noted; it is seen with particular force in the development of Marian devotion associated with the *Akathist Hymn* when it was introduced into the West. It is a known fact that, following on the Council of Ephesus, a flood of Marian devotions arose in the Eastern Church. One of these found expression in the Akathist Hymn, the most highly prized Marian Office in Greek Christian literature. Ritual prescribed that participants sing it in a standing posture; hence the name the "non-seated" hymn (a-kathistos). It contains twenty-four stanzas, whose initial letters are the successive letters of the Greek alphabet. The first twelve stanzas are narrative in character and deal with events from the childhood of Jesus; the second twelve, lyrical in form, acclaim Mary in accents of wonderment at her attributes. After each of two stanzas follow twelve verses (that is twelve times twelve), in which Our Lady is greeted, each preceded by the salutation HAIL (Chaire!): the theme constantly varying in content. The hymn found its way to Venice for the first time about the year 800. But it was not till the middle of the eleventh century, in keeping with the changed atmosphere prevailing, that hymns and chants of greeting to Mary appear in the West in growing numbers, modelled on the *chaire* verses of the Akathist, due allowance made for differences in treatment and selection. The most famous of these hymns of greeting is the *Salve Regina* which is traced back to bishop Adhemar of Monteil (d.1098). They led later to new forms of Marian piety and poetry. Whereas previous to the eleventh century only occasional prayers addressed to Mary were committed to writing and circulated, from now on prayers of the kind appear in great numbers. The favorite type is the salutation to Mary repeated in long sequences in praise or petition and mostly accompanied by an Ave Maria.

Litanies of Mary

An important, though obvious matter of note is the impetus which the *Akathist* lent to the development of the litanies of Mary. Dating from the twelfth century three drafts are extant which begin with Kyrie eleison and then record, one after another, Mary's titles of honor. They differ, however, from the verse structure of the *Akathist* chiefly in this: Instead of the *Chaire* which precedes each greeting of Mary we have an *Ora pro nobis* placed after it.

The Litany of Loreto whose origin has been recently traced to the sixteenth century is one of these. In the Paris manuscript, discovered by Meersseman of the 12th century, seventy-three eulogies of Mary are contained mostly in a two-line metric pattern; they were later shortened in various ways and again lengthened, but in essentials they are identical with the structure finalized in the Breviary of Pius V.

The Rosary

But the most precious and most enduring fruit produced by the Marian movement of the eleventh and twelfth centuries is the Rosary, which has remained to this day firmly linked with the Litany of Loreto. Along with the latter it derives its vitality from the angelical salutation as found in the Bible; a vitality further enhanced by roots likewise biblical in character; the Rosary is the Marian form of the Psalter.

Psalter for Layfolk

In our progress through the centuries of the Early Middle Ages we have recognized how stubbornly the Psalter was retained as *the* prayer book for the faithful. We have realized too that intermediary forms were necessary in order, on the one hand, to bring it more into line with Christian prayer, and on the other to keep it within reach of even the most modest worshiper. To this end it was given responsorial forms; it was supplied with headings that had Christian overtones; psalter-collects were introduced as accompaniments; abbreviated psalters were drawn up for lay people who were not qualified to tackle the complete Book of Psalms and were yet unwilling to forego the "Psalter." Finally, as in many cases such people were unable to read and could not be expected to use even the abbreviated psalter, rules were drawn up in the shape of the discipline of Penance which served as a substitute for the psalms. Instead of fifty psalms, a third of the three-fifties into which the Irish monks had divided the Psalter, a division which still survived, it sufficed to recite for the requisite number of psalms any psalm which one had mastered, with the addition or insertion of five Pater Nosters; and if that were not feasible one Pater Noster for each psalm was enough. The substitution of one Pater Noster for every psalm was provided for in the *Consuetudines Udalrici* (around 1080) for non-priests. The usual suffrage for the dead, which in the monasteries entailed the recitation of fifty or one hundred and fifty psalms, could, as attested to by numerous authorities, be fulfilled by those unable to read by the recital of as many Pater Nosters.

As indicated, the repetition of Pater Nosters constituted the first type of a Psalter substitute. If accuracy were to be guaranteed in computing, say fifty psalms, a counting device was needed. Around the year 1140 mention is made for the first time in the West of a string for counting prayers (such a device was already in vogue in the East). This was in the possession of a certain countess in the form of a *circulus gemmarum,* a string of pearls. A simpler type of string for counting must have been known earlier than the date mentioned. The most ancient representation we have is in stone and is of a counter with a division into decades of knots found on the grave of a certain knights-templar. That there was question here of reckoning the number of Our Fathers appears from the name given the string in various languages over the years, the *Pater Noster*, a term which partially survives today. In Paris the guild of patenôtriers plied a lucrative business, and in London one of its older streets is still called Paternoster Row. Similarly the technical term, the Pater Noster, meaning a rotating plant, is still in use. The Pater Noster psalter made up of one hundred and fifty or fifty Our Fathers must have been a familiar term everywhere for centuries. However, in the mid-twelfth century it was gradually supplanted by a Marian psalter which assumed various forms.

Marian Psalter

In the liturgical Office the psalms had a framework of antiphons which on feast days of Our Lady were given a Marian character. But about the year 1130 all psalms in the Psalter were furnished with accompanying texts of the same type: Each psalm had its choral stanza which started with a greeting to Mary (Ave, Gaude) and linking up with a word or a phrase from the psalm paid her a tribute of praise in ever-new variations. Fourteen such Marian psalters are known, dating from the twelfth to the fifteenth centuries, an eloquent testimony to the dynamism of this movement of piety, which combined fidelity to the psalms with an enthusiastic devotion to Mary, while releasing an astonishing output of lyrical expertise. A second step was taken in the course of the thirteenth century when the angelical salutation (and that of Elizabeth) often took the place of the psalm, while retaining the division of the Psalter into the three fifties. A further step was the composition of psalters of one hundred and fifty stanzas in praise of Mary which were no longer related to the psalms but began in each case with an Ave or Salve. This stanza-psalter which could be recited only with the help of a book was also out of the question for a large circle of worshipers, with the result that the stanzas also were dispensed with and the thrice-fifty Aves made up the psalter. A Rule of the Beguins published in Flemish in the year 1242 made the daily recital of three fifties obligatory under the name of the *Psalter of Our Lady*.

It was felt by this time that things had gone a bit too far in the way of simplification and possibly too that devotion to Mary, though it should be retained as a sound element in Christian piety, should not remain isolated. A report from the year 1243 informs us that not a few people were helped by the addition of a Gloria Patri to each Ave as was usual at the end of a psalm. Then likely enough the Paternoster-Psalter came to mind and a conjunction with it was sought. That the Our Father and the Ave Maria could be ranged side by side followed from the episcopal and synodal ordinances mentioned above. In the year 1226 the General Chapter of the Dominican Order, meeting in Trier, prescribed that the laybrother members, whenever they recited the customary Our Father should add to it the Hail Mary. The division into decades was probably taken over from the Paternoster-

Psalter. Thus by degrees the insertion of a Pater Noster after each decade of Aves came about.

Mysteries of the Rosary

Another embellishment, though late in gaining admittance, was the insertion of "Mysteries" from New Testament salvation history; these were recalled after each single Ave Maria and the holy name of Jesus was added; in this way the Marian Psalter was given a christological character. First attempts in this direction consisted in fixing for each Ave of a "fifty" a special clause, in most cases a short rhymed strophe; then the events of the childhood of Jesus, his life and passion were gone through. The pioneer in these efforts was the Carthusian Dominick of Prussia (d. 1461) who about the year 1429 introduced his fifty Ave-clauses. The decisive step toward simplification, the retaining of the same clause for each decade, was taken by the Dominican Alan of Rupe (d. 1475); he was also familiar with the division into the Joyful, the Sorrowful and the Glorious Mysteries. Only in regard to the naming of the two last mysteries in particular a certain hesitation was evident: it was only in the year 1500 or thereabout that the assumption and crowning in heaven of Our Lady were assigned to them, whereas up till then the general wish was for judgment and heaven to be stressed. This was in keeping with the wider horizon that opened up to view in those days and is being sought again today. Thus by the predominance of the purely Marian element in the Glorious Mysteries of the Rosary a time-determined factor was impressed on a popular prayer of a significance ranging beyond time;

much the same as in the Sorrowful Mysteries the physical sufferings of Christ were exclusively chosen for treatment.

The addition "Pray for us sinners" to the Hail Mary was made by the Carthusians about the year 1350; it took a long time to assert itself, receiving its definitive form along with the complete text of the Hail Mary in 1568 in the Breviary of Pius V.

St. Anselm

Among the spiritual men who contributed to the advancement of devotion to Mary in the eleventh century St. Anselm is to be numbered; its further evolution in the homage paid to the saints is also attributable to him. Among his works nineteen prayers have been transmitted to us, three addressed to Mary, ten to different saints, namely John the Baptist, Peter, Paul, John the Evangelist (twice), Stephen, Nicholas, Benedict, Mary Magdalen and the church patron. This long list should not tempt us to fear that Anselm, the pioneering theologian, had lost sight of the basic elements of Christian prayer: These prayers to the saints are of a special brand and do not differ essentially from his *Meditations*. We have the same inner tension between Christian sanctity and loftiness of soul on the one hand, and on the other man's futility and tendency to sin, a tension which is set forth with a verve proper to Baroque in ever-new terms and with plenty of hyperbole to spare. A saint is often given credit for results that God alone can bring about, like power to touch the heart or loosen the bonds of sin. The saint appears to be put on a level with the Almighty, when his mercy and that of an apostle are sought (misericordia Dei et Petri); Jesus and the beloved disciple are addressed together without more ado as Lord and lord (domine et domine); but then the petition for help is paraphrased unequivocally as *intercession* on the part of the saint. The prayer often meanders freely back and forth between the saint and God or Christ.

It is certain that Anselm encouraged devotion to the saints by the prayers he composed. Not that devotion of the kind was a novelty in the Church. The liturgical books abound in memorial days in honor of the martyrs. The tombs of the apostles and other great saints were the goal of many a pilgrim. Their relics preserved in costly shrines were the jealously-guarded treasure in many churches. Though such veneration was primarily an expression of wonder and awe before the fullness of Christian holiness, it must assuredly also have included the hope for protection and blessing. But formal prayers that went further in the direction of the request one might make to a fellow-Christian to "pray for me" were, as we have seen, only attempted with reserve. They may have become more frequent in this period; they appear especially in the form of hymns and songs. A monograph dealing with hymns to St. Peter goes to show the steady increase in the number of these hymns (Sequences, Tropes), one hundred and fifty-two of which are identified between the tenth and sixteenth centuries. The prevailing intentions for which help and intercession are sought have to do more with earthly and bodily needs. In this connection we may cite the Fourteen Helpers-in-Need to whom a brisk cult was paid in Germany since the fourteenth century. Looking back on the new era which began with the eleventh century and provided so many new spiritual insights and forms of devotion, we must first make a negative assertion—negative in as much as a twofold shadow cast on the religious world of those days now disappears. Two characteristic features of Christian piety which have forced their attention on us so emphatically in dealing with the history of the previous five centuries now gradually lose their influence. We allude to the disproportionate stress laid on the mystery of the Trinity and the exaggerated sense of sin which was then rife. In this connection the new theological thought which set in with early Scholasticism and especially with the Victorines may have played its part; and as regards a sin-complex the possibility of approaching the sacrament of Penance more frequently since the turn of the millennium acted as a liberating force.

Sts. Bernard and Francis of Assisi

These trends recede fully now and give place to the emergence of an astonishing balance and harmony personified in two figures in whom the aspirations and yearnings of the age found their fullest expression, personalities who cast their glow on the following centuries as well: Bernard of Clairvaux (d. 1253) and Francis of Assisi (d. 1226). A brief word of appraisal of each is called for. Common to both and the central feature in their spiritual outlook was the worship of the sacred humanity of Christ during his earthly life. Common to both also was the clarity with which the new spirit of piety could be seen to be rooted in Church tradition. In the case of each their contemplation of the human element in Christ circled continually about the two focal points familiar of old: the mystery of the incarnation and the mystery of the redemption, in their language the crib and the cross. This double theme also dominated the Church year with its calendar of feast days and as a result determined Christian thinking in general. The Christian of earlier centuries was indeed aware that salvation came only through the Godman who died for us and rose again, and that union with him was achieved through Baptism which has to be ratified and perfected only through a virtuous moral life. Now, however, this union is to be understood as a conscious imitation of Jesus, and our moral life as a personal, sympathetic response in fellowship of suffering, following along the road which the Savior first trod for us. Contemplation of the earthly life of the Lord was at once a contemplation and a proclamation of the ethical ideals of Christianity.

St. Bernard's first love, the favorite subject of his contemplation, was the childhood of Jesus and the Virgin Mary. He devoted thirty-one sermons to them. His admiring gaze is fixed on Mary's humility, purity and lofty dignity; the name *Domina nostra* (Our Lady) which soon became her most popular name was his invention. Then too his entire thought and prayer turn about the name of Jesus, apart from which all else remains insipid and without relish. The crannies in the rock mentioned in the *Canticle of Canticles* (2:14) he finds in the wounds of his Lord in which alone he hopes for safety and repose (Sermon 61); the sufferings and painful treatment meted out to him are the sachet of myrrh (Cant. of Cant. 2:14) which he will carry on his breast forevermore (Sermon 63). It is not so much Christ's physical sufferings that claim Bernard's attention but rather the condescension and self-effacement of the Godman. These fire Bernard's enthusiastic love, a love which soars above all that is of earth to reach the love of the Supreme Uncreated Good.

As for Francis of Assisi, it suffices to point to Greccio and his celebration there of the crib during the Christmas of 1223, and to the five wounds of the redeemer which he received on his body on that night of ecstasy on Mount Alverno, to become henceforth himself a living copy of the crucified. Among the prayers and writings attributed to Francis is an Office of the Passion after the model of the Little Offices. It covers the seven Horae of the day, each consisting of a "psalm" structured mainly on a free selection of verses from different psalms, concluding with a Gloria Patri and framed by a Marian "antiphon" which remains always the same. The psalm itself is so constructed as to give expression to the voice of the suffering redeemer in the genuine spirit of the Church liturgy of the passion. But as in the case of the seraphic saint it is the events of Christ's earthly life and their reproduction in his own life that serve as a first step to his soul's elevation, to that perfect type of adoration which has found such glorious expression in his *Song of the Sun*.

7
The Gothic Era

The great achievement of the High Middle Ages was the Theology of Scholasticism. It influenced in its own way the prayer life of the period. As in other fields, so too in the theology of prayer, Thomas Aquinas holds a foremost place among its classical interpreters. Less important for our purpose are his efforts to reach a clear-cut definition of prayer. His predecessors had defined prayer as an elevation of the soul to God, a self-surrender to God, a movement of the mind toward God; Thomas is at pains to safeguard before all else the role of the intellect without, however, defining the notion in set terms. We are more interested in the statement he makes in connection with St. Paul's remark in his letter to Timothy (1 Tim 2:1) that prayer in every case must include an ascent of the mind to God (oratio), confidence in God's mercy (obsecratio) and gratitude for favors received (gratiarum actio); then it can pass over to supplication (petitio).

St. Bonaventure

With Bonaventure, the Franciscan theologian, we

have a direct approach to the religious movement of the period. St. Francis's meditations on the passion he carries forward in his writings which are interspersed with prayer. In the *Vitis Mystica* (Mystical Vine) Christ is shown as the true vine wounded sorely by the dresser's knife, bound fast to its supports, the vine whose blossom sheds abroad a precious fragrance, under whose foliage we can find shelter. In the *Lignum Vitae* Christ is the tree of life growing apace, advancing in suffering, to be crowned eventually in glory.

A work often attributed to Bonaventure, though its real author was another member of the Franciscan Order, the *Meditationes Vitae Christi* develops the same theme further, depicting with imaginative skill individual scenes from the life and passion of Christ and adapting them to the mentality of the people. He then points to the place that these themes occupy in the structure of the spiritual life. In the *De Triplici Via* (the Triple Way) he deals with the doctrine of the Three Ways, the purgative, illuminative and unitive of the pseudo-Denis and confirms that "The Way of Illumination consists in following in Christ's footsteps," a following which covers his earthly career and includes the veneration to be paid to his mother. Thus the way lies open for the stage of perfection where love for the uncreated, Supreme Good triumphs, and prayer is pure adoration.

Though a clear distinction is made theoretically between the Ways, the seraphic doctor is as fully aware as the spiritual teachers of the following centuries that in practice they must dovetail and interlock one with the other. He stresses that the thought of Christ's passion is of the greatest significance in advancing along the Way of Purgation.

German Mysticism

Apart from the religious movement at work in the newly-founded religious orders, the teaching and example of the great masters and standard-bearers of piety during the High Middle Ages were particularly operative among the spiritually-advanced section of the people of God, kindling a new fervor for prayer. We refer to the movement toward mysticism during the later Middle Ages and especially to its German variety. It spread through the monasteries, finding its way also to the layfolk chiefly through the mission sermons of John Tauler (d.1361). The chief features of German mysticism, especially in its representatives from the Dominican Order (men like Eckehart, Tauler and Suso) consisted in a searching for God based on interior recollection, in an effort to break loose from all that is bound up with the senses and the creaturely, in order to find God within the soul, seeking closest unification with Eternal Wisdom and Divine Love.

In clear contrast to this "speculative mysticism," the mystery of Christ and Christian revelation in its totality are brought out in much bolder relief in the mysticism of the Cistercian Nuns in Helfta. They combined a solid theological training with an inner warmth in the manner of St. Bernard. Their outstanding representative is Gertrude the Great (d.1302). With an extraordinary fidelity to the ruling of the liturgy she follows the course of the ecclesiastical year in her devotions. Absorbed in the mysteries of the Life and passion of her Lord, she dwells with special love and affection within his pierced heart, that heart which for her is a tuneful lute, a censer from which unceasing adoration mounts to the Most Holy Trinity. We have here the harbinger of devotion to the Sacred Heart of Jesus, which even to our day manifests in model form the entire order of salvation and gives it a coherent unity. A similar sense for the whole is evidenced in her "Exercitia", Days of Recollection of a sort, which she composed for her nuns. They consist of fervent prayers based each time on a definite theme, starting with the renewal of the grace of Baptism in terms of the baptismal rite, and concluding with a preparation for death. The prayers are addressed indiscriminately to God or the Man-Christ or the Holy Spirit, to Mary too, and yet never lost their orientation to the totality of the Christian mystery.

New Religious Orders

In this period the refined standard of religious culture and the exalted life of prayer which prevailed in the monasteries still kept them worlds apart from the general mass of Christians. Nonetheless, the latter were now beginning to be influenced to a greater degree than in earlier times by monastic practice. This influence was exerted mainly by the new Religious Orders of St. Francis and St. Dominic whose chief activity lay in the popular missions they conducted. The effect they produced can be seen in tangible form in the tens of thousands who flocked to the Lenten sermons of Berthold of Regensburg (d.1272), or when Bernardine of Siena (d.1444) as herald of the holy name traveled through Italy and made the symbol I H S the common property of the faithful.

Third Orders

But the echo of this missionary activity found its main expression in Third Orders, associations of layfolk who, though remaining in the world, were anxious to share in the life of religious. These associations were able to link up with already existing groups of an "Order of Penance." Francis of Assisi himself joined such a group when in 1207 he broke with his family. Members of these groups led a life of comparative retirement and under Church guidance observed certain rules regarding fasts, mode of dress and practices of prayer. Now, under the auspices of the two Religious Orders mentioned, and with their active encouragement, these groups began to flourish, and soon their membership grew apace. In addition there existed confraternities of various kinds but more loosely structured than these and unconnected with the Orders. On a religious basis these bodies carried out different tasks, mostly in favor of the neighbor, like nursing the sick and caring for the poor. From the fourteenth century they were closely affiliated with one or other of the guilds, lending them a religious character and often even merging with them. Further, it was precisely in the domain of these confraternities that individual centers of devotion emerged, where such had not already been the purpose of their foundation. In later centuries in the closing period of the Middle Ages this religious trend is characteristic of subsequent foundations. Thus we have the Confraternities of the Passion, of the Blessed Sacrament and especially those associated with the Mother of God, including the Confraternity of the Rosary founded around 1470 which was destined to have a spectacular future. An impetus was also given to the veneration of the saints by the guilds, each of which chose as patron a saint associated with some symbol of its profession: For example, the guild of tailors took St. Martin as patron, that of the coppersmiths took St. Vitus Martyr. Their memorial day was marked at least by a Liturgy.

Their Prayer Life

Now, we may ask, what was the prayer of these lay groups like? We have to distinguish various gradations, differentiated not only by the degree of fervor accompanying devotion but most of all by the level of education to which their members had attained. Those who could read and even understand some Latin were in a position to nourish their piety from the psalms as in earlier centuries. But now there was no longer question of the entire Psalter nor of the Office recited in church; there was question rather of that selection from the psalms which had been added to the Office since the ninth century, and which now appeared chiefly in the shape of the Little Offices. In this way there came into existence the Books of Hours, *Livres d'Heures,* of the thirteenth to the sixteenth centuries, many hundreds of which are still preserved in our libraries. These were the prayer books of the later Middle Ages. They were usually embellished with miniatures and were often of such tiny format that they could conveniently be carried in a pocket in one's belt. In addition to the Penitential Psalms, the litany and selected prayers as well as excerpts from the gospel, they usually contained the Little Office of Our Lady and the Office for the Dead, both of ancient date and both additions to the choral prayer of the monasteries since the turn of the millennium. Further Offices now emerged, drawn up in a similar pattern to the foregoing and, like them, without reference to the ecclesiastical year and often much abbreviated: Such were the Offices of the Holy Cross, of Christ's Passion, of the *Compassio* of Mary, of the Blessed Sacrament, of the Incarnation, of the Trinity, of the Holy Ghost, Offices also in honor of all saints or of particular saints like John the Baptist, Magdalene, Catherine or of a patron saint. Indeed the more these special themes were stressed the greater was the shift from the psalms to the "trimmings" or accessories that framed them. This was especially true of rhymed Offices that served the purpose of private devotion to such a degree that the psalms themselves threatened to disappear altogether.

The Office of the Passion of Christ was held in especially high regard; it often served as a daily prayer, a privilege otherwise reserved for the Office of Our Lady. Though in some books of Hours it is missing, still the miniatures depicted in Our Lady's Office, true to venerable tradition continued to treat of the stages of the passion up to the Vesper-Scene, an expression in vogue today for the taking down from the cross and the Pietà when Christ's Body is laid on his mother's lap, themes appropriate to the hour of Vespers. On the other hand the Horae arrangement of the Office of the Passion was so vividly recalled in later times that in devotions to Christ's sufferings and even in the reading of the passion the division into seven sections was maintained. A *"Prayer of St. Gregory"* on the passion in seven parts, seven invocations each followed by a Pater Noster and Ave, was widely disseminated. Seven was seen as a symbolic number.

Toward the end of the Middle Ages the Book of Hours appeared also in the language of the people as was the case in England around the year 1400 when the *Prymer,* the Book of Hours in a typical format, constituted the layman's prayer book. Later it appeared in print also and ran into many editions.

Spiritual Reading

It must have been roughly the same circles whose piety had been nourished by the Book of Hours who were now in a better position to round off their religious development by the reading of spiritual books, just as the psalmody of monks and clerics was supplemented by an extensive programme of reading. For now there existed a devotional literature which appealed to the people, not wide in compass but for all that well disseminated. We have mentioned already the *Meditations vitae Christi.* Of a similar type but much wider in range was the *Life of Jesus Christ* composed by the Carthusian Ludolf of Saxony (d.1370) which retained its popularity for two centuries. The growing interest in lives of the saints was met by the *Legenda Aurea* of Jacobus de Voragine (d.1298) which was translated into all the languages of the West, and still survives in countless printed editions. Preoccupation with death, which was current in the closing Middle Ages with their Dances of Death was met by booklets which the *Art of Dying* (ars moriendi) was expounded. That such literature stood in good stead those who could not read is illustrated by one of the nine sayings attributed to Albert the Great since the mid-fourteenth century: "If you read aloud something worthwhile to a person it is more agreeable to me than if you were to eat and drink nothing but bread and water for seven years."

For some time, however, these book-aids did not touch the great mass of the people. Even members of Third Orders were in the main immune from their influence. This is clear from the prescriptions for prayer drawn up for them. The *Regula Tertianorum sive Fratrum de Poenitentia* composed in Florence in 1284 differs in no respect from the Rule for the Poenitentes issued in 1215. This prescribes that clerics, that is persons who are conversant with the Psalter, are to recite the canonical Horae; the *illiterati* say, in place of Matins, twelve Pater Nosters and Glorias, and for every other Hora they say seven such. At Prime and Compline those who "can do it" add the Confession of Faith and the *Miserere mei, Deus*. Further, all should attend Matins in their parish church during Lent, before Christmas and before Easter. In a rule of more recent date daily attendance at Mass "if they can conveniently do so" is mentioned for the first time. The extra prayers prescribed for the different associations of Tertiaries and the Orders of Knights (which stood on the same footing with them) varied in detail. But it was always with the help of the Pater Noster, (to which the Ave Maria was added with a certain hesitation) that the substitution was made. Only the numbers changed: By multiplying seven for the Little Hours they jumped to fourteen for Vespers and to twenty-eight for Matins. In the German Order of Knights, if non-clerics happened to be present at the choral Office, they were expected to carry out these same duties.

Devotional Life

It appears that the prayer life of the simple folk remained at the same level as heretofore, or it may have been more modest still. Their most important duty was attendance at Mass on Sundays and Holydays of obligation which were many (on an average one a week) and if possible on working days too. This consisted of reverent attention to the important parts of the Holy Sacrifice; the Pater Noster and the Credo were said at the consecration and—a point of special importance—eyes were fixed in adoration on the Sacred Host at the elevation. A sermon was heard; an opportunity to do so became more frequent after the Mendicant Friars were founded. The ecclesiastical year was followed and duly observed. Honor was paid to the saints who by their patronage helped the people to shoulder the cares and worries of daily life. Their relics were venerated, especially when they were exposed to view on feast days in the hope, sometimes superstitious, of obtaining blessing and protection.

Corpus Christi Processions

But it was the Blessed Sacrament exposed which riveted in powerful fashion the eyes of the beholder in a fresh excess of faith. The less often people ventured to receive Holy Communion (even in the rules of the Third Orders provision was made for its reception only three times a year) the greater their desire to gaze upon the Sacred Host, at least with the eyes of the body, and in that way find a substitute for its sacramental reception. Increased opportunities had to be found for this both within and without the Mass. A special receptacle for the Host, the monstrance or ostensorium, was introduced. In 1246 the feast of Corpus Christi was inaugurated and propagated, and from the year 1277 onward the Corpus Christi procession, which became an object of popular devotion in a big way. It soon absorbed the whole apparatus of earlier processions and finally the tradition associated with parades through countryside and city street. In many places scenes from the older passion-plays were enacted in which live performers spoke their parts in the form of drama, and thus came into being the Corpus Christi Play. In the later Middle Ages these religious plays became an important factor in the spiritual life of the people; thus the mystery play as Passion and Easter Play, the Advent and Christmas Play, the Epiphany Play, or even a play glorifying a patron saint. For whole months long the entire population of town or village was under its spell. It is reported from Frankfurt on the Main that in 1498 a Passion Play lasted four days and that two hundred and fifty persons performed in it.

This fervor in reconstructing the earthly life of Christ was not, however, matched by a similar consciousness of the Savior's sacramental presence or his indwelling in the soul of the Christian. Popular piety lived more at a surface level than at the center of the gospel message. It was threatened more than in former times by superstitious practices shown particularly in an excessive trust in relics, in the punctilious performing of a set number of devotional practices and in the gaining of indulgences, bogus in some cases. Church blessings too, which in the later Middle Ages were pronounced on all and sundry and were meant to lend a religious consecration to life, were all too often the object of exaggerated expectations, thus constituting a peril to the faith.

The penchant for the numerical fixing of forms and objects of devotion referred to was symptomatic of the peripheral and of extreme elaboration which traditional ways of piety had reached. The numbers five and seven played a large part in this trend: the five wounds, the five joys of Mary, the seven words spoken on the cross, the seven falls, the seven (or five) bloodlettings, the seven (or five or fifteen) sorrows of Mary. Each of these objects of devotion had its special prayer assigned to it. Added to these was the homage paid to the individual members of Christ's Body and to his "Weapons" (the instruments of the passion). Finally, the later Middle Ages were familiar with a devotion to the Seven Places of Refuge: the Blessed Trinity, the sacrament of the altar, the cross, Mary, the angels, the saints, the souls in purgatory—a devotion which attempted to bring unity to the multiform.

Surface Piety

The tendency to dwell on the periphery and to indulge in excessive elaboration, appears most of all in devotion to the Mother of God; a devotion expressed in terms of sympathy with her in her sorrows in *Compassio*, in a mourning with her which survives to this day in the *Stabat Mater*. The Pietà depicting the virgin holding the dead Christ on her lap was the most cherished image of her in the epoch under review. Veneration was extended to her mother, St. Anne, whose cult became the prevailing "fashion" of the closing years of the Middle Ages. A favorite theme of late Gothic art was the motherhood of Anne, depicting her in company with Mary and the Child Jesus. Devotion to Mary suffered an eclipse of a sort when in the fifteenth century the *Te Deum* was recast and figured, in its opening line, Mary as *Te matrem laudamus*. More than that: Attempts were made to give a theological justification to the hightide of the Marian cult, as did Richard of St. Lawrence (d.1260) when he suggests that the Son of God had made over half of his kingdom to his mother, namely the prerogative of mercy, reserving that of justice to himself.

We see from the above what little contact popular piety in the late Middle Ages had with the central facts of the Christian order of salvation. The only explanation for this is that the official liturgy of the Church had become an unknown quantity to the rank and file. In the monastic churches and in the numerous collegiate churches in which the clergy were obliged to divine service only, a resplendent liturgy was conducted. Day in, day out, echoed and re-echoed in the churches the recitation of the Office (mostly sung,) culminating in the conventual service. But the liturgy was a matter for the clergy only; even on Sundays and Holydays of obligation, as for the layfolk, only their presence was possible. Not that they took umbrage at this. They contributed in their own way to the liturgy by building the churches. In the cities the burghers offered cathedral and minster the money needed and the expertise of their architects and artists. Rich endowments supplemented continually donations already bequeathed. New collegiate churches with their colleges of priests were founded with the purpose of having divine service celebrated in them. The underlying idea in all this, dating back to the period when the monasteries conducted their *laus perennis*-service, was that communities of priests and monks should represent the faithful in glorifying God and thus drawing down his blessing on town and country.

But at this period even clerical divine service itself had in large part succumbed to inertia. We hear of abbot Garcia Cisneros (d.1510) of Montserrat instructing his monks to meditate on the successive events of the life and passion of Christ while reciting the psalms of the choral Office, which goes to show that little or no spiritual nourishment was to be derived from the psalms themselves. In 1534 Cardinal Quinonez issued a new Breviary with a wealth of Scripture readings but abridged as far as the psalms were concerned. It met with wide acclaim. Despite this a Spanish conciliar theologian before the Council of Trent condemned it on the grounds that Scripture was an affair for theologians only; for the ordinary cleric, *idiota clericus* who had not advanced beyond the Latin Grammar, for the *vulgus clericorum* (the clerical crowd) an extensive reading of the Pauline Letters was worthless; their job was the rendering of the psalms and no more, which goes to show that this type of service had become a purely external affair. The psalmody in the form and dimension then current no longer awakened in the soul of the worshiper the echo it had formerly done. It was natural then that the best spirits of the age looked to new ways of approaching God.

8
Passage to the Modern Age

The new movement which took its rise with Gerhard Groote (d.1384) in the Low Countries was called the *Devotion Moderna*. It was, as its name indicates, eventually meant to mark the contrast in which it stood to the ways of piety formerly practiced. It purposed to point a way to God more adapted to the contemporary age. The Church at the time was rent by schism; the individual Christian was left to his own devices; the liturgy pursuing its course from earlier days and estranged from a changing world had lost its buoyancy and had little to offer the searching soul. Even the traditional discipline of monastic Rule, as experience proved, was powerless to hold captive the spirit of former days. The theological speculations which in German mysticism had once more with Ruysbroek attained to a high level were beyond the reach of the simple Christian in his quest for God. In such circumstances the Brothers of the Common Life and the Canons of Windesheim associated with them, while remaining faithful to Church tradition, sought a straight-forward path to God unencumbered by superfluous accessories. They prayed the Office, yet without special solemnity or additions like the Office of Mary or the Office for the Dead. They met for daily Mass, a low Mass devoid of show or display.

Devotio Moderna Piety

The prayer they adopted in order to renew and sanctify their lives was interior prayer. This too they took over from present tradition. It had been invariably recommended as the pith and marrow of the *lectio divina*. It had been the consistent aim of the monks in their withdrawal from the distractions of the world in order to find God and to rest in him. Had not St. Bernard both by word and example worked to that end?

But for this interior prayer (and herein consisted the new approach) a firm support was now sought and a certain systematic order to ensure its stability and cohesion. This seemed all the more necessary as the contemporary world with its revolutionary ideas, its message proclaiming a new order of things, and a liberated humanity which looked to the ancient world for its inspiration, called for a parallel support and anchorage.

This order of procedure was determined on the one hand by fixing definite material for interior prayer, and on the other hand by offering suggestions and counsels regarding the manner in which it should be conducted. Gerhard Groote had pointed to two themes in particular with which prayer should deal: the Last Things and the Life and Passion of Christ. His disciples and those who came after him adhered to this programme in their daily or twice-daily meditations and developed it further in their own writings. Sketches for meditation matter were drawn up and assigned for prayer throughout the week, following roughly a liturgical arrangement: on Fridays and Sundays themes from the Lord's passion and the joys of heaven respectively were treated, and on the early days of the week the childhood and the public life of Christ or (as with abbot Garcia Cisneros) the Last Things, death, hell, judgment. Soon the weekly schedule was operated with greater latitude: septenaries (sets of seven points) were drawn up irrespective of the days of the week, as in the *Formula Exercitiorum Spiritualium* dating to the second half of the fifteenth century which proposed as subjects for meditations six sets of seven points, they treat successively of God's benefits, the seven joys and sorrows of Mary, the sufferings of Jesus, the life of Jesus, the Last Things, the angels and saints; but a warning is added that on Church feast days the mystery of the day should be observed.

Rules are also set forth for the method to be followed in mental prayer rules meant as helps not restrictions. They touch the need for previous preparation of the matter and offer hints on how the meditation should begin and how it should end, not omitting prayerful colloquies. In the main all this is conformable with ancient tradition. In the *Scale Meditatoria* of John Gansfort (d.1489) with its many steps, regulations had already reached the stage of over-elaboration.

Movement toward Reform

The best known exponent of *Devotio Moderna* piety is the book *Imitation of Christ*. True, it treats with winning simplicity of compunction of heart in face of God's supreme grandeur, as also of the Last Things, term of human life. But apart from the opening chapters there is little mention of the following of Christ which has given its name to this famous book. We miss most of all any emphasis on what was the essence of the *Devotio Moderna* since the days of its founder, namely the will to work for reform in the Church. As a fact the representatives of the movement hoped, and not in vain, that the persevering cult of interior, personal prayer in which the keypoints of the Christian order of salvation were reviewed could not fail to have its effect one way or another, for example, on a religious who was drifting along in a careless, thoughtless way of life: he would come to his senses or else quit the monastery; in either case a distinct advantage for the monastery in question. Toward the end of the fifteenth century a strong movement toward reform was felt throughout the Church, a reform which affected the religious Orders especially and sent its ripples as far as Italy and Spain. This was due to the new insistence on mental prayer. The Benedictine monastery of Montserrat with its abbot Cisneros is only one example of this, though the best known one.

Ignatius of Loyola

It was at Montserrat that Ignatius of Loyola too received the first stirrings which were to have such a decisive influence on his future. Subsequent to his stay there and to the long months of prayer at Manresa, he drew up the plan of the *Exercises*, committing them to writing and later (up to 1535) giving them a final redaction. These Exercises were only a logical, systematic follow-up of what had long been practiced in *Devotio Moderna* circles. The great themes to which in the

Ignatian *Exercises* the exercitant applies himself in mental prayer are divided into four "Weeks." A first week is assigned to meditation on sin and the Last Things; the following weeks to the life and passion of Christ up to his glorification. These point the way along which we are to follow the Master. What is new in the *Exercises* is that Ignatius in his second series of meditations proposes the call which Christ the King continually issues to all men to follow him in the struggle to spread his kingdom here below; and (in the course of further exercises) an invitation is extended by the Eternal King, to those so disposed, to embrace poverty and perfect humility. The original purpose of the Exercises was to serve as an introduction and a help in choosing a state of life in accordance with the divine Will, and in a given case to opt for a life of selfless labor in promoting the kingdom of God. A further extension of the Exercises, in favor of Christians living in the world, was the *Retreat* made in common and conducted by a priest who proposed the matter for prayer. But certain adaptations first had to be made, and these were laid down in 1500 in a "Directory to the Exercises."

"The Spiritual Exercises" as a School of Prayer

Among the methods of mental prayer given in the Exercises, the Exercise of the Three Powers of the soul, as the author terms it holds a conspicuous place. An object, accessible to the senses, is chosen for consideration and presented to the memory and reflected upon by the intellect with a view to practical resolves. Each exercise should begin by placing oneself in the presence of God in a prayerful attitude and should conclude by coming back again to him in a genuine personal encounter. Ignatius is aware of and recognizes other methods of mental prayer, for example prayerful reflection on some definite theme, or on a prayer text which one turns quietly over in one's mind in order to relish its savor. And to conclude the Exercises, and as the obvious crown and culmination of all that has gone before, he sets the "Contemplation for Obtaining Divine Love" in which the soul is caught up in a simple regard of all the benefits he showers on his creatures.

What was experienced in concentrated form in the *Exercises* was meant first and foremost to be operative as a school of prayer in the Order which Ignatius founded. Mental prayer was to be a first priority in the prayer life of the Jesuit and the mainstay for his apostolic activity. As we saw, meditation in one form or another had always been part of the life programme of a religious Institute but was regarded as subsidiary to choir prayer which stood first in importance. The monasteries and other religious associations influenced by the *Devotio Moderna* had already provided a definite framework for mental prayer, assigning it a suitable place beside the choir prayer, as for instance at Montserrat in conjunction with Lauds and Compline. Similarly the Dominicans at the General Chapter in 1505 made mental prayer part of their daily programme as did the Franciscans.

Place of the Divine Office

In St. Ignatius' Order mental prayer was placed first, thus shifting the center of gravity of the spiritual life. Not that the Office was dispensed with (though this would not have been altogether unthinkable in the then prevailing legislation) but it was thought desirable, as in the case of other religious bodies of the period, to confine the Office to private recitation, a practice which in the meantime had become fairly widespread. The purpose in view was to have more freedom for apostolic work, and the "service of the neighbor."

As is known, the Society of Jesus met with great opposition in pushing this point of its programme. Owing to the attitude adopted by Paul IV and again by Pius V the decision was seriously questioned. A matter of principle was actually involved here; though it was scarcely spoken of in such terms. Was the solemn choral prayer to be maintained and cherished simply as a service rendered to God, with no questions asked about the greater or lesser spiritual benefit of him who takes part in it or any edification and spiritual fruit otherwise accruing? Must a special value be assigned to it as if it were a sort of *opus operatum* independent of the interior dispositions of the person engaged in it? Or could a retrenchment be made in favor of an alternative manner of praying which specifically included one's inner involvement and so offered greater prospects of personal enrichment and stability? At least where any loss involved in such retrenchment could be compensated for, and more than compensated for by apostolic activity?

A decisive answer to this question was not forthcoming owing to the more or less general view that the Church in its totality had in the traditional formal *Officium Divinum* a prayer of its own and had commissioned monks and clerics to perform it. Here too the idea of substitution had won through and had linked up with the definite notion that the Church was a quasi-persona (a sort of person) and as such must have her own form of prayer—a centrally controlled one—to be differentiated from the prayer of the faithful and of individual churches throughout Christendom. The idea of prayer "in the name of the Church" which is implicit in this was unknown to St. Thomas, though recognized and appreciated by the Jesuit theologian Suarez. It played a role in the Second Vatican Council and found its echo in the Constitution on the Liturgy.

It was no wonder then that the withdrawal of a religious Order from choir prayer in the sixteenth century met with such an unfavorable response. It could not be denied that the private recitations of a prayer meant to be said at community level and in public could only be a solution dictated by necessity. It lacked that sense of completion which communitarian recital could have lent it, as also that aura of reverence and nearness to God which choral chant guaranteed, even when the mind failed to grasp the meaning of the words uttered.

Apostolic Activity

A second question intervened on the first. The New Order of the Society of Jesus was from its inception geared to work for souls. Must not this objective give a special coloration, if not a stamp of its own, to its prayer life also, and especially to its mental prayer? The question became an actuality in Spain, the home of a new and flourishing mysticism, in a century too which gave the Church a Teresa of Avila and a John of the Cross. Was it desirable that in the Jesuit Order a method of prayer should be fostered in which man, penetrated by a lively sense of his creaturehood, should make it his sole aim to return to God, concentrating all his energies on attaining to union with, and repose in him? Such was the aim of the anchorites and the entire world of ancient monasticism, an aim which must remain a lofty ideal in the Church in all ages, for those at least who wish to abandon the world and find God more surely. Fr. Mercurian, the third successor of St. Ignatius as General of the Order gave an answer in the negative sense by a practical measure he promulgated: Among a list of spiritual books meant for the young Jesuits he excluded the writings of the modern mystics, among others Tauler and Ruysbroek. Mercurian's successor, Fr. Aquaviva, in a communication addressed to the members of the Society in 1590, was more explicit: Contemplation too is a good thing, he agreed, but the love of God enkindled in contemplative prayer must remain oriented toward him. In the interests of such service a Jesuit must be ready at all times to forego the delights of contemplation. True, in the seventeenth century a formal school of prayer emerged within the Order, inspired by Cardinal Bérulle's movement, in which contemplative prayer had a predominant place. Louis Lallemant (d. 1635) was its best-known representative.

But there was to be no shift in the Society's purpose: Work for the kingdom of God in the world and not a life of contemplation in the cloister. The prayer of the Jesuit, if it was to be integrated with his life, must keep in mind the ways and fates of the common man, not soar in rapid flight above the paths of purgation and enlightenment. It must above all seek to follow Christ's example during his life here below, using that model as a yardstick of spiritual progress and zeal for souls. Accordingly the manner of piety fostered in the Society of Jesus from its beginnings had a practical trend, as was clear from the very aim of the *Spiritual Exercises:* "to put one's life in order." That did not immediately mean asceticism and activism as two distinct functions; for this orienting of one's entire life had to proceed from within. In view of its essential mobility the Order could not, to the same extent as older religious bodies, build on the stability guaranteed by well-organized community houses; rather its hope for permanence must be grounded chiefly on a rule of life as set forth in the earthly career of Christ. So too with the Society's activity in a world whose structures were beginning to disintegrate, a new stabilizing factor could only be hoped for from an appraisal of the facts and laws of the Christian faith leading to a new order of things and to a rejuvenation of life as the result of a method of prayer which was close to life. With this fresh orienting the Society of Jesus began its task, a task destined soon to envelop wide circles of the contemporary world.

The Reformation

Other factors, too, influenced the religious outlook of the nascent epoch. The storm of the Reformation and the pitiless criticism directed by its adherents against traditional ways of piety were bound to have a sobering effect on the Church, despite the exaggerated forms in which those criticisms were framed. The Council of Trent adopted measures to combat obvious abuses, for example those connected with the granting of indulgences and the cult of the saints. The heat with which the struggle was carried on, the necessity to repel unjust accusations and to safeguard spiritual values which brooked no surrender, led to an insufficient appreciation of the positive good contained in the movement, namely insistence on a simple essentially biblical form of piety. At all events results were to be discerned in many prayer books of the period which tried to base their contents on texts of Scripture, the writings of the Fathers and authors of repute and actually cited their sources on occasion.

Influence of Humanism

The Humanism too of the period exerted an influence on prayer and the literature connected with it. It managed to stamp certain features of its spirit on the Liturgy in the form of new hymns and the improvement of older ones along classical lines. Thus the prince of humanists, Erasmus of Rotterdam, not only composed works of a religious nature, including the *Enchiridion Militis,* but also prayers which attained to a certain vogue. An important representative of the Catholic reform, Georg Witzel (d.1575), himself author of a popular prayer book, regarded Erasmus' Commentary on the Pater Noster as the best of such productions known to him. However, Erasmus' bitter criticisms of the externals of traditional piety, of certain forms of life in the cloister, of contemporary theology as well as his outlook on the world which was more pagan than Christian, hindered the salutary effect which his humanism was calculated to produce.

St. Francis de Sales

It was only later that the genuine ideals of Humanism in the field of piety were realized in the person of St. Francis de Sales (d.1622). He adopted a positive attitude to the world, to its beauty and its pleasures. Though conscious of man's frailty, he sees him renewed in Christ rather than in his fallen state; Francis is the herald of Divine Love. He instructs his Philothea how to remain united with God in the midst of worldly affairs. Apart from morning and evening prayers, there is little mention of vocal prayer in the *Introduction to the Devout Life* dedicated to her but he does insist on daily mental prayer according to a simple method and on the practice of interior recollection. The impact made by Francis de Sales on his generation endures to our day.

9
Religious Sentiment in the Baroque Era

The Council of Trent had brought clarity to certain disputed questions in the area of dogmatic theology and had worked toward the restoring of an ordered system in the liturgy. As to the further domain of Christian piety it had been content to remove any glaring abuses that might have crept in. But to inaugurate a new religious mentality and a return to fundamentals, presuppositions were lacking at the time of the Council, most of all a proper historical perspective. The result was that the cleavage between liturgy and the people remained as before. In the reform of 1568-1570, it is true, the liturgy was freed of some of the accretions of the Middle Ages, and the introduction of rubrics prevented it from growing unchecked again; but in its central processes it remained obscure even for the clergy. The faithful had made the best of it by their reverent attitude at the divine service. We read of Ignatius of Loyola that he was daily present at Vespers and Compline when at Manresa in 1522-1523, though he knew no Latin, and that during High Mass celebrated each day he usually read the story of the passion.

Nevertheless, following on a directive from the Council, efforts were made to give the people some instruction on the Mass. This was frequently done through the medium of prayer books in Latin, sometimes indeed in very detailed fashion; the worshiper was led step by step from the prayers at the foot of the altar and the Introit to the concluding prayer and the final blessing. For this suitable texts were available. In other prayer books one was content with a general lead and possibly some prayers to be said at the elevation of the Host. The actual purpose of the prayer books of the period was not to serve as an aid to the celebration of the service, but rather as material for the extra-liturgical prayers during it and as preparation for the reception of the sacraments.

After Trent

In the epoch following on Trent Christian piety in essentials simply continued the traditions inherited from the Middle Ages. A significant feature here was the multiplicity of its forms. All devotions which arose in the past continued to flourish or were further developed. Devotions to the Blessed Trinity, to the Person of the Father, to Eternal Wisdom, to the Holy Spirit, to Christ's agony in the garden, to his five wounds, to the angels, to Mary and to her sorrows and joys, to the Fourteen-Helpers-in-Need, to relics and to special saints. These devotions were kept alive in the confraternities and pilgrimages, in the old and new prayer books. Naturally such a variety made the spiritual life unduly complicated. This is apparent in certain texts for morning prayer when the different heavenly powers are to be approached, one after another. Among these devotions a preferential place was occupied by the passion of Christ.

Despite this dispersal of spiritual energy however,

a pronounced effort at concentration is also evidenced. In devotion to the saints, that paid to the Mother of God, in whom the mystery of the Incarnation is so vividly brought to our minds, comes more and more to the fore. The tide of criticism unloosed by the Reformers on the cult of the saints breaks in vain on devotion to Our Lady which is strenuously defended not alone by the apologists. A question put by visitators to parish priests of doubtful orthodoxy, for example, ran: "Do you regard the Ave Maria as a prayer?" (not only as a greeting). While in earlier days, apart from the Holy Land, pilgrimages were made chiefly to the shrines of various saints, like Santiago de Compostella, Martin of Tours, or to the graves of the apostles, sanctuaries of Mary arose in the sixteenth century in many places which then became pilgrim centers. The Marian Rosary not only maintained its place as the most favored form of prayer but assumed new variants. The so-called *Salve Devotions* too (an inheritance of the Middle Ages), took on new embellishments: In the different monasteries, first, and then more generally, the *Salve Regina* was linked to one of the canonical Horae, usually Compline. This occurred on a definite day of the week, like Saturday or on one of Our Lady's feast days, and on every day, somewhat later. The choir of the monks or of the clerics repaired to the chapel of Our Lady and there on their knees sang the ancient antiphon with Versicle and Oratio.

In the long run this ceremony came to be regarded as a special devotion of its own, in which the layfolk took part with growing interest. As early as the fifteenth century a number of charitable endowments were founded in order to promote it; so that in parish churches too the same devotion was maintained. The local teacher with his pupils had a contract to ensure that the Salve Regina was sung there regularly. The "Salve" became the origin, even the nucleus of a popular evening devotion on Sundays and feast days as the name Salve Devotion (salut in France) indicates; even today in many dioceses it functions as an afternoon or evening devotion.

Devotion to Mary was further reinforced by certain prayers which were recommended to the faithful for daily recitation, to the extent of dislodging even more important themes. One such recitation was the Angelus. In the fourteenth century it was customary on the ringing of a bell in the evening to recite the Ave Maria three times, a practice recommended by various synods. More, a signal was given frequently at morning, noon and evening to remind people to pray, so that the early Christian tradition of dwelling on the Way of the Cross at definite hours had not entirely died out. Simon Verrepäus in his popular *Enchiridion* mentions the ringing of a bell in the evening as a reminder to recite the Angelical Salutation in memory of the Incarnation; with the midday signal however he associates the death of the Lord and with that in the morning the resurrection. An instruction issued by Bishop Echter of Mespelbrunn in Wurzburg in 1584 insists that the bell at midday should relate to the memory of Christ's passion, leaving the Ave to be said at the morning and evening hours. As early as 1520, however, in other localities the ringing of the bell three times daily was brought into relation with the Mother of God.

Jesuit Sodalities

Sodalities for students founded and directed by the Jesuits whose purpose like that of previous associations for example, the Confraternities of Divine Love, was to foster a fervent spiritual life, chose, if not at the beginning at least very soon, the Virgin Mary as their patroness. Here there was an obvious stressing of the Marian element though this was not the immediate purpose of the sodality. Before admission into the sodality the candidate recited a prayer by which in the traditional language of the oath of allegiance in feudal times he promised loyal service to his high protectress (domina, patrona et advocata). In the first draft of the Rules in 1564 sodality members were obliged to recite daily the Office of Our Lady or the Rosary. In some cases a condition of admission was enrolment in the Confraternity of the Rosary. In the seventeenth century many sodalities of Our Lady, in order to promote her honor, vowed under oath to work toward the definition of the doctrine of her Immaculate Conception. Great care was taken, especially in the early days of the sodality, to maintain a normal Christian balance in religious practice.

The trend toward a middle course is still more discernible in regard to the Sacrament of the Altar. Despite the suggestion of the Council of Trent that when the faithful attended Mass they should not confine themselves to a "spiritual Communion" (*spirituali affectu:* session 22, 6) the accent still remains on the permanent Sacrament of the Altar, the honoring of Christ really present in the tabernacle. Medieval tradition inculcated also a certain reserve. To receive sacramentally was an action out of the ordinary and meant Holy Communion outside the Mass, either before or after it. However, during the later Middle Ages frequency of reception was somewhat on the increase. In a regulation promulgated in 1587 for the sodality, Holy

Communion could be received on the first Sunday of each month and on the chief feasts of the Church Year. Yet Fr. Coster in his *Libellus Sodalitatis* issued about the same time already advocates the rule to communicate spiritually each day during Mass and sacramentally once a week. But for the general public, the average reception of Holy Communion was still confined to a few of the greater feasts in the course of the year.

Worship of the Blessed Sacrament

Reserve in approaching the altar was, however, more than compensated for by the zeal with which the Blessed Sacrament was worshiped. The practice, inherited from previous centuries, of exposition, especially during Mass, was maintained chiefly in the northern countries. Tabernacle and High Altar are closely interrelated and become the center-piece of the church fabric; not infrequently indeed a special throne for exposition is erected above them. Blessing with the Sacred Host terminates the Sunday afternoon devotions and in many localities is given the name of Benediction (Benedizione). A climax in the worship of the Eucharist is the Forty Hours Devotion. Originally this devotion was intended as a special way of honoring the period during which Christ's Body lay in the Holy Sepulchre. (The Blessed Sacrament was often placed in a tabernacle representing the sepulchre, the Altar of Repose.) In 1527 the Forty Hours Devotion was more and more divorced from its original setting and raised to an independent rite, primarily as a propitiatory devotion in calamitous times. Then the Forty Hours took on a definitely reparatory character as a protest against the Reformers' denial of the Real Presence. At the same time, through the external pomp (rich scenic effects and musical décor) associated with the devotion, it mirrored popular thinking and that festive joy characteristic of the Baroque Age. At first the devotion was confined to Jesuit churches but it soon spread to the parishes. From the seventeenth century onward the "Great Prayer" or the "Perpetual Prayer" was often conducted the whole year through, from parish to parish in a diocese.

The emphasis laid on these two focal points of religious life, namely devotion to Mary and the worship of the Eucharist, is significant for the period with which we are dealing. Devotion to the Mother of God in the presence of the Blessed Sacrament exposed seemed a happy combination of both.

Sacred Heart

With devotion to the Heart of Jesus the mystery of Christ found another mode of expression. The Carthusian Joannes Landsberg published in 1536 the Revelations of St. Gertrude of Helfta. But a wider publicity was achieved through the movement inaugurated by John Eudes (d.1680) and Margaret Mary Alacoque (d.1690). From the beginning the devotion met with considerable opposition: The object of veneration allegedly was but a section of Christ's humanity and an arbitrary one at that. Even as late as the year 1729 the Congregation of Rites refused to accord it canonical sanction. In 1765 however the Polish hierarchy was given permission for a feast of the Sacred Heart of Jesus. To do justice to the devotion the religious situation prevailing then in regard to the worship of Christ must be kept in mind. The veneration of the cross with its full theological implications which flourished during the first millennium of the Christian era had been replaced more and more by a sympathetic contemplation of Christ's physical sufferings and had been fragmented as well into particular devotions which, like the popular Way of the Cross stopped short at the sepulchre. An exact parallel to this we find in the realistic representations of the crucified common to Gothic and Baroque art which, otherwise than in Romanesque art, in their portrayal of the suffering and dying Christ scarce allowed the dawning glory of Easter to shine through. From this impoverishment sprang, with a certain necessity, the desire to find a formula, a symbol in which once more the totality of the Mystery of Christ in its winning features, in a love which only asked for a return of love, could be expressed. This symbol was the heart of the Savior, a symbol more readily grasped in that epoch than in ours.

It is no accident that following in the wake of the new religious movement and linked with the Easter cycle of the ecclesiastical year a new feast could arise for each of the two christological central points, Corpus Christi and the Heart of Jesus. The first of these became in many countries *the* feast of the year (the Fête-Dieu in France, the Herrgottstag in German-speaking lands), while the latter did not continue to meet with full public recognition.

In general the traditional forms of the liturgy were observed with scrupulous fidelity for the Church feasts, some of which were celebrated with a great display of pomp, often in splendid new buildings and to the accompaniment of an inspiring church music. But popular piety, eager to share in the joyful fervor which such displays offer, seeks and finds its nourishment mainly in the new types of devotion which arise in such varied profusion. Triduums or novenas are celebrated by way of introduction to favorite feasts or serve as days of intercessory prayer for important intentions. Community marches to gain some spiritual favor, and solemn processions are so much in vogue that the Baroque period has been called (by A.L. Mayer) the *Age of Processions.* Religious plays attained to a new flowering in more countries than in Calderon's Spain. Community prayer too, not catered for by the liturgy, finds a new form of expression in the Litanies, a novel type of the responsorial psalmody. In the year 1600 a *"Fasciculus Litaniarum"* was issued in Munich; it contained thirty-three litanies inclusive of those of the Divine Persons, of various aspects of the redemption, of the Blessed Virgin, of saints of different categories. Some were expressive of praise, others were petitions for various intentions. Though Rome issued certain restrictions and prohibitions (during public service only the Litany of all saints and the Litany of Loreto were allowed) still the Litany remained the favorite devotion of the period, with its didactic and biblical background, with the possibility it offered of heaping up metaphors which catered for contemporary taste, and its potential also to create fresh musical forms.

Prayer Books

In its layout the litany is a prayer for the community but its literary location (so to speak) is the prayer book which is chiefly meant to serve the needs of the individual user. Since the invention of printing and the days when reading became an almost universal accomplishment, the prayer book gained a massive importance. In the early days of the printed prayer book collections of prayers were not the only material provided, as for instance in the *Hortulus animae,* successor and heir to the medieval Book of Hours. An essential feature in the makeup of these printed prayer books were the different day hours whose structure betrays their origin in community choral prayer though in general they dispense with psalms and retain only their framework.

Both litanies and day hours are combined and given a new lease of life in a prayer book the *Coeleste Palmetum* of Fr. William Nacatenus, S.J., which since the year 1660 has had a wide circulation and has survived to the present. In addition to the Office of the Blessed Virgin and the Office for the Dead (in the versions fixed by the Roman Breviary of 1568) it contains for every day of the week "short day hours with their accompanying litanies and prayers." Each of the day hours include the seven Horae, and each of the latter consists of hymn, "antiphon" and oratio only.

Nicatenus' *Coeleste Palmetum* can also be regarded as a typical example of post-Tridentine prayer books: not only do they contain a varied assortment of prayers, prayers for Mass, Confession and Holy Communion: they offer also instructions on how to hear Mass and receive these sacraments. Two methods are proposed for attendance at Mass; the first is to follow step by step its various stages by the recital of special prayers; the second is based on meditation on the passion. A novel feature in the prayer books composed by Nicatenus and by many other Jesuits was the detailed instruction given on the spiritual life and most of all on methodical mental prayer. It may be noted that when Louis of Granada, O.P. (d.1588) like Ignatius of Loyola started to introduce lay people to the art of meditation he met with opposition. Since those days, however, the value of such procedure had been publicly accepted: meditation was zealously fostered in the sodalities of Our Lady and elsewhere; Fr. Francis Coster's *Libellus sodalitatis*, which was issued in many editions since 1586, contained seven draft meditations on Christ as Model of the Virtues.

It goes without saying that not a few of the devotions mentioned, as well as the day hours and litanies, being readily available in the new prayer books were utilized for community prayer during the regular meetings of the Confraternities and Sodalities. This holds also for the sections dealing with mental prayer. In due course both types of religious practices found their way from these smaller communities to the parish afternoon services. Definite mention is made of mental prayer being held at them in many diocesan parishes like those of the Rheinland, a custom which prevails to the present.

Meditation Manuals

For the purpose of mental prayer a special genre of literature in the shape of meditation books was created, mainly the work of the Jesuits. These manuals carried on what the *Devotio Moderna* had initiated, but on a larger scale. Not confined to septenaries of meditation matter they followed the course of the ecclesiastical year and the gospels read during it.

Francis Borgia (d.1572) was the pioneer in this type of literature. Meditation books by Nicolaus Lancicius (d.1633), Nicolaus Avancini (d.1686) and especially Louis de Ponte (d.1624) enjoyed a wide circulation. Four hundred editions and more of the meditations of the last mentioned were issued and are still in use today.

Here we have an earnest effort to deepen the religious life of the period and within certain limits to link up with the liturgy. Further steps were taken in promoting liturgical practice and in advancing Christian piety by a movement which concentrated on mental prayer in a manner of its own. Pierre de Bérulle (d.1629), later Cardinal, was from his early days overmastered by the notion of man's creaturehood and his utter dependence on God. The extreme example of this dependence he had glimpsed in the self-effacement of the Word made flesh, whereby the Godman had become the Perfect Adorer.

The Oratory

This inspired Bérulle to give his institute the name of *Oratory*, the Oratorium of Jesus Christ, Highpriest. It was not long before a sturdy religious movement affecting a growing circle of the French clergy was born of the Oratory. The *Mysteries* of Christ's life formed Bérulle's favorite theme for contemplation in which inner attitudes (états) were the chief concern. In view of our union with Christ by grace our life must grow more and more conformable with His image until it becomes a single act of adoration of God. To achieve this goal the path one must traverse is by way of a ceaseless self-abnegation and a total offering of oneself (adhérence) to Christ. Detailed prescriptions are offered for the practice of mental prayer. Two things are recommended: Acts of adoration at its beginning and a sharing in the dispositions and the mind of the Incarnate Son during its progress. In this way one's spiritual life becomes fully integrated. It has been said that Bérulle introduced a "theocentric revolution" in that he brought to honor a type of prayer which does not occupy itself with individual acts of the intellect and resolutions of the will but seeks simply to grasp God's reality in the hope that a renewal of one's workaday life will be the spontaneous fruit of the process. Bérulle's successors in the Oratory, Charles Condren (d.1641) and Jean Jacques Olier (d.1657), the latter the founder of the famous Seminary of St. Sulpice, continued to develop the master's ideas; they originated the "French School" of the spiritual life.

Olier shows how in the Blessed Eucharist we can contemplate the self-effacement of Christ. There especially we have a model of how we should think, and act. His favorite prayer, still in vogue today, runs as follows: "Come Lord Jesus, live in your servant in the fullness of your power. . . ." Olier was probably one of the first to recommend visits to the Blessed Sacrament. True, he exceeds due measure in extolling the priest's dignity, and he bears some responsibility for fostering a too eschatological concept of him when he asserts that, like Mary, he shares in the power of the Eternal Father in begetting the Son. It is not surprising that in circles where adoration was maintained as basic to the spiritual life notable efforts were made to restore contact with the liturgy. Pierre Lebrun, (d.1729) author of a Commentary of the Liturgy, in four volumes, was an Oratorian. As is known, the New Gallican Liturgy was the fruit of these efforts which, in the main, were quite othodox.

Further Developments

On the other hand this movement of piety, so exclusively oriented to the central mystery of Christianity, gave birth to extensions of a peripheral character which could hold their ground only with difficulty. Bérulle had stressed the childhood of the Godman, his helpless childhood, as the first stage in his career and the prime example of his self-effacement. Thus a peculiar emphasis was laid on Christmas, to such an extent that his disciples started to develop special devotions on the twenty-fifth day of each month in honor of the Divine childhood. Jean Eudes (d.1680) brought the idea a step further: A favorite theme of Bérulle's contemplation had been the life of Jesus as lived in Mary. From the moment of his incarnation he had been dwelling within her, determining her entire thinking and willing. This was now the chief feature of Eudes' piety. On one occasion he designated Jesus simply as "the Heart of Mary." In 1643 he introduced into the Oratory, with the approval of his bishop, a feast of the Heart of Mary. Later on, in 1673—again as the first to do so—he planned to add a feast of the Heart of Jesus. Eventually he combined both hearts, invoking both in a common greeting: "Hail most loving Heart of Jesus and Mary." The fairly numerous religious societies which unite in their titles both Sacred Hearts draw their inspiration from this school of thought. In another direction Bérulle's ideas found a fresh development in the so-called relationship of slave (esclavage) to Mary, a type of piety which was at first rejected by Rome but on further clarification was approved. Grignon de Montfort (d.1716) regarded it as the foremost means of assimilation with Christ and spread it as *True Devotion to Mary*. It consisted in doing everything through Mary, with Mary, in Mary and for Mary.

There have been saints who under forms and images such as these gave expression to the love of God which fired their hearts. Of similar high purposc arc those religious institutes which recognize in those holy men and women models for their own striving. But we can well understand that in their regard the Church adopted at first a policy of reserve, and that viewers from without who had no appreciation of the flame that burnt within, became their severe critics. Also, it is not difficult to discover in the origins of Bérulle's *Oratory* reasons why the movement was not attended with greater success, due allowance being made for the opposition it had to contend with owing to contemporary circumstances. It was a form of piety which had been structured on the mystery of the Incarnation in too one-sided a fashion: The Easter mystery, the risen Christ and the Church which he gathered about himself are left on the fringe of its horizon. That "Farewell to the Middle Ages" which Bremond prized in the movement was not achieved.

10
Further Reflections

The centripetal efforts in the life of religious belief at the beginning of the modern age had safeguarded, systematized and further developed the valuable gains inherited from tradition. But they failed to affect what was most central, the liturgy. This remained a world apart, sacral but inaccessible. In contrast to the Middle Ages the Baroque period was at a disadvantage inasmuch as the multiplicity of forms which previously was allowed a measure of free play had now been largely stablized and found itself on the defensive.

Jansenism

The result was that the critics had plenty of areas for their attacks. Bérulle's theocentric piety in one of its side developments had become involved with pessimistic notions current in certain of Augustine's writings and had since 1640 developed into the Jansenist heresy. This doctrine taught that man is incapable of good; only by the greatest effort could he, with God's grace, hope for salvation. Hence a rejection of all newer forms of piety that catered to human weakness especially devotion to Mary and to the Sacred Heart, and a call to return to primitive Christianity, as these innovators interpreted it. In another direction, but with a like rejection of later forms of piety, the theocentric tendencies were driven to extremes by the representatives of Quietism and the "Pure Love" movement.

Catholic Extremes

Since the year 1652, within the Church itself, a discussion was being carried on with reference to Marian devotion: On the one hand in order to defend it against Jansenist attacks, and on the other to warn against any exaggerated forms of it. From the latter point of view a well-meant caution contained in the writing of an unnamed "German Catholic" (1674) met with opposition. It was the same with a criticism by the famous Ludwig Anton Muratori who published in 1747 his "Balanced Devotion of a Christian." Muratori condemns the many novel devotions which were constantly cropping up and inveighs against the hagiographers who ascribe bogus miracles to the saints. He attacks, too, the externalizing of religion, superstitious practices (for example the placing of an image of Christopher on the church wall), exaggerations in the homage paid to Mary, the notion that every grace presupposes a special intervention on her part, as held by the "Slaves of Mary." He sketches a picture of divine worship in keeping with the basic tenets of Christianity, points to the one mediator between God and man, and offers an introduction to the proper manner of joining in the Mass. He combines with all this many practical counsels, for example the Sundays should not be overlaid by saints' feasts and there was need of a popular prayer addressed to Christ. Muratori was vigorously attacked in counter publications, despite which Benedict XIV took the author under his protection.

Alphonsus Liguori

At about the same time, without being too critical of existing conditions, and desirous of countering the harshness and rigor of Jansenism, Alphonsus Liguori sought, in his prayers, sermons and widespread writings, to foster among the Christian people an esteem for prayer and for its zealous practice. His foremost endeavor was to introduce, as material for reflection, traditional themes like the Blessed Sacrament and the Virgin Mother, and use these as a lever to raise the faithful to a genuine love of God. Muratori was well versed in the old Roman liturgy. In France the liturgical tradition had been highlighted by the labors of the Benedictines of St. Maurus, particularly by Mabillon (d.1707) and Marténe (d.1739). As a result the main features of divine service and piety as practiced in early Christian times were disclosed; but at the same time fresh weapons were put in the hands of critics of the established order. The Gallican bishops had felt justified, accordingly, in making various improvements of their own in the traditional Roman liturgy. From 1680 onward books of this new Gallican liturgy made their appearance and gave gradual currency to it in France. Some pastors, too, without demur based their divine service on the newly discovered models and without asking questions restored to their people their share in prayer and chant.

German Enlightenment

In Germany also after the mid-eighteenth century a vigorous criticism was raised against traditional forms of piety and church service. It was determined less by considerations of history; its origins lay rather in the Enlightenment which had dominated the thought of the period, chiefly on the Protestant side. While vindicating the claims of reason, the movement was pushed too far and led to an excessive rationalism, so that all that remained of religion was a frigid Deism, for which Christianity served as a cloak in the circles which adhered to it still. The outward show which was maintained in this way, coupled with the justifiable claims of reason, resulted in the movement making definite headway among leading circles of the clergy and finding sympathetic support there. Thus it was in the Electorates of West Germany and at the Synod of Pistoia. The secular power then took a hand with Josephinism, which not only suppressed the contemplative Orders within its jurisdiction but forcibly abolished such manifestations of traditional piety as were incorporated in pilgrimages, tertiaries and confraternities.

Not all the objections of critical reason, however, should be faulted. The positive ideas of reform, for example, developed by the Pistoia Synod regarding divine service anticipated in a whole series of points reforms which were carried into effect in the Catholic Church before the Second Vatican Council. Faulty, however, was the rationalist approach of the movement and its arbitrary mode of procedure; faulty its biased views on doctrine and life in the Christian context; faulty too was its irreverent attitude to established forms of piety, even though these might have been inadequate in the circumstances. On the other hand, it was opportune to take cognizance of the rights and laws of nature which were coming into greater and greater prominence through a fresh scientific approach and to find a place for them in the religious field as well, checking by them the norms and forms of Church liturgy and Church pronouncements, thus restoring to corporate worship the leading position it once had in the life of piety. It was indisputable that there was much in popular piety, especially in the matter of pilgrimages and the cult of the saints that not only lay on the very periphery of Christian reality but also harked back to a world view that postulated a continual intervention of God in the details of our earthly pilgrimage, an intervention, moreover, that was all too directly linked with specific saints and sanctuaries. Given the growing knowledge of nature processes, such a view could no longer be sustained, indeed it was already out of date with a large section of the Christian people.

It was a difficult situation for those men who could appreciate the current situation. On the one hand they were anxious to rise to the demands of the times, and on the other they had to counter the inroads of rationalism. Not all of them succeeded in reaching a balanced solution. Wessenberg, Vicar-general of Constance during the years 1802-1813 lacked the poise characteristic of his Dillingen teacher Johann Michael Sailer (d.1832). Though Wessenberg's undoubted merits were fully recognized, a critic described his ideal as "classicism in the religious field" reminding him of a church decorator who, in an elegant attempt to cater to all tastes covers its walls with a dreary uniform whitewash unrelieved by color, with nothing for ornamentation but straight lines (C. Groeber). Sailer without indulging overmuch in polemics, indicates in his *Pastoral Theology* a sure path for priests in care of souls and the possibility "in present circumstances" of bringing the faithful to an intelligent sharing in the Sunday service (with the help of printed translations, prayers to be recited aloud and suitable hymns). The prayer books he composed were also of assistance to simple souls: Omitting much redundant matter they concentrated on the larger issues of Christian thinking and praying.

The Reaction: Traditionalism

Apart from the effects of its negative criticism the age of Rationalism left few enduring traces as regards religious belief. The revolution to which it gave birth was an interlude which was followed by a reaction in the literal sense of the word. *Traditionalism* which in matters of religion refused to acknowledge any competence to the intellect and regarded tradition alone to be valid was the theological expression of this reaction, just as in the realm of art the Neo-Gothic and the Nazarene group of painters were symptomatic of the period. In the field of piety, then, in the nineteenth century and beyond it, the current traditional devotions, among others the cult of Mary and the worship of the Blessed Sacrament and the Sacred Heart predominated. They were zealously fostered, given a sound theological basis and evaluated as far as feasible. Each had its own month assigned it, without much attention being paid to the ecclesiastical year.

The Rosary

The most popular expression of piety at this period was devotion to the Mother of God. Leo XIII in sixteen encyclicals and apostolic letters on the Rosary sought to enhance the fruits of a devotion which in its developed form reaches far beyond the Marian element.

The Real Presence

The most august object of worship in a Catholic church was the Blessed Sacrament preserved in the tabernacle, exposed for adoration on the high altar and raised aloft in blessing. It can be said in effect that, generally speaking and without making many distinctions, God's presence and "God's House" became terms identical and co-extensive with one another. In the numberless religious associations of Perpetual Adoration which arose chiefly in the nineteenth century a new *laus perennis* was ushered in, this time muted but all the more interior. In them all, as in so many focal points, the flames of divine love were enkindled. And since the year 1881 International Eucharistic Congresses have highlighted the glorification of the Blessed Sacrament in a new way. At the Munich Congress in 1960 a telecast version of the programme was issued for the first time, lending a broader basis to such international gatherings.

Devotion to the Heart of Jesus attained to its full significance in the nineteenth century, as is evidenced by the large number of new religious foundations which emerged under that title. The spiritual importance attached to the devotion is emphasized by the practice of Consecration to the Sacred Heart which reached a widespread popularity. In some particular forms like that of the *Enthronement of the Heart of Jesus* a tendency is clearly evident to lend the symbol of the Divine Heart the importance which the cross had during the first millennium of the Christian era.

Though the liturgy was duly celebrated with punctilious accuracy, an attitude of reverent aloofness was maintained in its regard. Aids to its accessibility, however, increased in number toward the end of the nineteenth century. *The Holy Church Missal* by Anselm Schott, O.S.B., which appeared for the first time in 1884 is typical of its kind. An effort was also made to justify the claims and significance of Divine Service in a foreign tongue and therewith the Latin choral prayer, for the benefit of men and women ignorant of that language.

Attempts at Reform

Prerequisites for a renewal of the liturgy itself and for ensuring its central position in Christian life had first to be created in the nineteenth century. And they were in fact. Due to a revival of theology, based on orthodox thinking and a sense of history, a secure foundation was once more guaranteed for the faith in order to combat the inroads of rationalism. Historical studies, Christian archaeology and a return to the Fathers brought tangibly nearer the life and piety of the ancient Church. To combat unbelief a more intense study of the sources, especially Sacred Scripture, was imperative. The apostasy of entire sections of the Christian population, especially those affected by rising industrialism, showed finally the absolute need of re-examining forms and methods obtaining in church life. More, it became clearer every day that the accepted order of things in many points was just that of the Middle Ages and not at all an essential expression of Christian revelation. Fundamental truths of the supernatural order, like the mediation of Christ, the Church as the people of God, the Mystical Body, grace as a new life—all these had but a shadowy existence in the consciousness of the average Catholic.

It was due to external circumstances that the breakthrough occurred in the domain of the liturgy. It could just as well have happened in that of the gospel-proclamation, for instance, in the matter of catechetical reform. The renewed impetus given the liturgical movement is linked with the Belgian Benedictine Lambert Beauduin, a former worker-priest and with the year 1909. It had a long pre-history: It started with the renewal of monasticism and its concern for the *Opus Dei* (the Office) inaugurated by abbot Prosper Guéranger (d.1875). Other factors intervened, like the interest of academic circles in the soul-stirring rendering of the Choral Office in the abbeys, and a fresh interpretation of the nature of the Church which was the chief merit of the Catholic Tubingen school. The movement coincided with the Catholic Youth Movement during the period between the two World Wars. It spread rapidly to the parishes, first by way of interest in the prayers said by the priest at the altar, then by way of sharing in prayer and hymn in a more or less organized way, or in the case of church buildings in the form of new designs for church interiors and liturgical vestments. In the *Mediator Dei* of 1947 the movement scored its first if limited success. Then since 1950 and definitively with the *Constitution on the Liturgy* of the Vatican Council in 1963, the entire liturgy was reorganized on a planned, conscious basis.

Clerical Piety

It was perhaps far from clear in the beginning that this breakthrough in the liturgical sphere was bound to be operative in the whole range of the sacred ministry and the spiritual life. This was immediately true only of a part of the liturgy reform, namely that concerning clerical piety. In the Code of Canon Law (c.125) clerics were expected to spend some time daily in mental prayer, to visit the Blessed Sacrament and to honor Mary by the recital of the Rosary, and all this in addition to the full Office in the form of the Roman Breviary. If the cultivation of mental prayer in some form or other has to be regarded as a *must* for the spiritual life, what of the obligation of the Breviary? History has made it clear that this latter, especially in its traditional range and form, spelt a burden suited, indeed, for the shoulders of contemplative monks but not for those of priests engaged in apostolic work.

If the obligation were to stand, then this Office must be brought into harmony with conditions obtaining among the clergy, thus ensuring its proper functioning. For that the dialogue forms of choral prayer (greetings, petitions for blessing and the like), forms too which had significance only in sung parts, would have to be dispensed with. The Breviary must be reduced to relevant proportions, and an arrangement of the Horae be recognized which was in keeping with the day's press of work. Before all else a type of Breviary had to be found which would enable the user to fulfill his duty of praising God and to cater for his spiritual nourishment and edification as well.

The importance of the Breviary itself and of the Psalter in particular could not be called in question. Since the close of the millennium, it is true, we find a growing withdrawal from the psalmody as accepted from the fourth century onward. But, as in the words of the apostle, "we do not know how to pray as we ought" (Rom 8:26), and as our human weakness has to be buttressed in some form or other by prayers prepared in advance, there remains no other guide, at least for the cleric who can read, comparable with the words of Scripture, especially those of the Psalter. While in vocal prayer we dutifully follow the way it leads us, we have the best ground for hoping that by the word of God, offered us in wise discretion by the Church, heartfelt prayer will be continually enkindled.

Still the decisive field in which an innovation was bound to be introduced had relation to the Eucharist—decisive for clergy and layfolk alike. And here there was question of a changed attitude to the mystery. Pride of place was now given the celebration of the Eucharist (no longer its mere cult). The course was already set in 1905 when Pius X issued his Decree on *Frequent and Daily Communion* and asserted its obvious necessity for the Christian life. This was now stressed by the incorporation of Holy Communion in the Mass itself. The homily was also reintroduced and the faithful were brought closer to the altar by communal prayer and chant and thus drawn into relation with the sacred event. The stage was reached when it became clear that the Rite itself, and finally the language of the Mass, must be adapted to the people of God. Here the Council took the decisive steps.

Life of Prayer in the Modern Age

In the first centuries of Christianity, as we have seen, the faithful had, apart from the celebration of the Eucharist, an organized life of prayer, sanctioned by the Church. This comprised the prayers said in their homes as well as those said at church meetings. Does this not suggest a norm which is valid for all time? The Second Vatican Council mentions celebrations of the Word of God which should be held with the people, at least on certain days, for example those preparatory to a feast day or introductory to Advent and Lent or supplementary to and, in given circumstances, substituted for the Sunday Mass. All this is a pointer to the revival of what the Horae of Matins and Vespers recited by the people stood for in ancient times and acts as a spur to restore Vespers at least to a more popular form.

During the last centuries a call to prayer in the home, to "daily prayers," to morning and evening prayers and prayer at meals, has been repeatedly issued by pastors of souls. *Pace* the moral theologians, they have made a sort of precept of it, as may be seen in the formula for examining one's conscience prior to going to Confession. But a fixed schedule has not been drawn up for daily prayer: This would be an impossible task, given all the circumstances that have to be taken into consideration and the variety of material that can be offered. When, moreover, in Catholic countries the

Angelus Bell still rings out, as it used to over village and city, three times a day, its call is only seldom understood and answered in the traditional way.

Prayer Books

In modern centuries a support for the personal prayer of the faithful, private prayer as well as communal said at church gatherings, has invariably been the *Prayer Book*. The variety in which these books were issued increased, if possible, in the nineteenth century. Then an effort was made to link them more closely with the liturgy. This is manifest in the special editions of Missals and Vesper Books brought out in France for parish use, and in Germany in the Laymissals already mentioned, which soon swamped all other prayer books after the breakthrough of the liturgical movement.

One type of prayer book alone vies in circulation with the Laymissal, if it has not already passed it: the diocesan Prayer-and-Hymn-Book proper to German territory. Its origins date back to the eighteenth century. Efforts within the Catholic Enlightenment to push the liturgical movement had led to an intensified fostering of musical chant during divine service. Starting with the "Catholic Hymn Book" of Speyer (1768) hymnals soon appeared, mostly in the dioceses of the Rhineland, with supplements containing prayers suitable for afternoon devotions. Thus in the course of the nineteenth century a Song-And-Prayer Book, or a Prayer-and-Song book was issued at the instance of the bishops in most of the dioceses. These ran into hundreds and thousands of copies. And so the multiplicity of private prayer books, not all of them dictated by an enlightened piety, yielded place to a single volume destined to become the liturgical book of the faithful, one which incidentally guaranteed church approval for their private prayers. When in the years subsequent to 1930 the Liturgical Movement began to assert itself in the very structure of the Book even a clearer diocesan character was given it. For all intents and purposes it now contained within its two covers everything needed for divine service, at least on Sundays and Holydays. Efforts were now chiefly aimed at the creation of a national Standard Prayer Book by selecting elements common to the various diocesan prayer books, which in any case had been oriented in a similar direction.

Conditions Today

Christian prayer has had to face difficult shocks in our day. Many of the factors which impelled our forbears to pray have lost their relevance. The laws of nature rule the world. And God Himself is pushed out to the furthest edge of reality, so that many regard prayer as outmoded and redundant. A skepticism which spares nothing and erodes the foundations of the faith undermines even the desire to pray. Others, in their satisfaction with the new order of things, have adopted an attitude of caprice and indiscipline which, likewise, can only end in religious impoverishment.

On the other hand prayer has also gone through a refining process. The incense of adoration and thanksgiving rises today all the purer from hearts that have remained steadfast. Worshipers all the world over forgather in Holy Church with souls uplifted in the love of the Spirit, to him who has gone before us and is our Highpriest, in praise of the Creator whom in fullest confidence we call our Father.